Humanizing Distance Learning

Humanizing Distance Learning

Centering Equity and Humanity in Times of Crisis

Paul Emerich France

A SAGE Publishing Company

FOR INFORMATION:

Corwin

A SAGE Company

2455 Teller Road

Thousand Oaks, California 91320

(800) 233-9936

www.corwin.com

SAGE Publications Ltd.

1 Oliver's Yard

55 City Road

London EC1Y 1SP

United Kingdom

SAGE Publications India Pvt. Ltd.

B 1/I 1 Mohan Cooperative Industrial Area

Mathura Road, New Delhi 110 044

India

SAGE Publications Asia-Pacific Pte. Ltd.

18 Cross Street #10-10/11/12

China Square Central

Singapore 048423

Program Director and Publisher: Dan Alpert

Senior Content
Development Editor: Lucas Schleicher

Associate Content
Development Editor: Mia Rodriguez

Production Editor: Tori Mirsadjadi

Copy Editor: Diane DiMura

Typesetter: C&M Digitals (P) Ltd.

Proofreader: Dennis W. Webb

Indexer: Maria Sosnowski

Cover Designer: Scott Van Atta

Marketing Manager: Maura Sullivan

Printed in the United States of America

Library of Congress Cataloging-in-Publication Data

Names: France, Paul Emerich, author.

Title: Humanizing distance learning : centering equity and humanity in times of crisis / Paul Emerich France.

Description: First edition. | Thousand Oaks, California : Corwin, [2021] | Includes bibliographical references and index.

Identifiers: LCCN 2020043223 | ISBN 9781071839058 (paperback) | ISBN 9781071839065 (epub) | ISBN 9781071839072 (epub) | ISBN 9781071839096 (pdf)

Subjects: LCSH: Distance education—Aims and objectives. | Humanity. | Educational equalization.

Classification: LCC LC5800 .F73 2021 | DDC 371.35—dc23

LC record available at https://lccn.loc.gov/2020043223

This book is printed on acid-free paper.

20 21 22 23 24 10 9 8 7 6 5 4 3 2 1

CONTENTS

ACKNOWLEDGMENTS

In my last book, I did a poor job of centering and acknowledging the contributions of voices of color to the education field. It wasn't until I watched a webinar through Haymarket Books, featuring Gholdy Muhammad, Bettina Love, and Dena Simmons, where they reflected on the fact that white people in education cite white researchers, theorists, and educators disproportionately, in turn, erasing the contributions of People of Color and specifically Black theorists and researchers, that I looked back through my book and saw that I was, in fact, guilty of this, as well.

As a result, I want to start by acknowledging this fact and the many researchers, theorists, and educators of color who have contributed to a significant change in my thinking over the course of the past year. You will notice many of them cited in this book. These individuals include Bettina Love, Ijeoma Oluo, Kimberlé Crenshaw (who I inadvertently left out when talking about intersectionality in my first book), Ibram Kendi, Austin Channing Brown, Ta-Nehisi Coates, Liz Kleinrock (@teachandtransform), Gloria Ladson-Billings, Rich Milner, Britt Hawthorne (@britthawthorne), Tiffany Jewell (@tiffanymjewell), Layla Saad, Naomi O'Brien (@readlikearockstar), Dena Simmons, Joy DeGruy, Zaretta Hammond, Gholdy Muhammad, Chimamanda Ngozi Adichie, Kenneth Jones, James Baldwin, Kevin Kumashiro, and the Conscious Kid (@theconsciouskid).

I did not do a poor job because the resources created by these educators were necessarily hard to find; I did a poor job because I did not make a concerted effort to seek them out. Maya Angelou tells us that when we know better, we must seek to do better. This is a first step for me in trying to do better.

I also want to thank my friend and editor, Dan Alpert, for encouraging me to engage in the continuous process of finding my voice as a writer. Writing this book was a joy, and it was undoubtedly because of working with him. I also want to thank Senior Content Development Editor Lucas Schleicher and Associate Content Development Editor Mia Rodriguez for their camaraderie in this effort, as well as Carol Ann Tomlinson, Ron Ritchhart, and Rich Milner for reviewing and endorsing the book.

And finally, to my first teacher—my mom. Thanks for teaching me to love books and for showing me how to treat everyone kindly, with the respect and humanity they deserve. I love you!

ABOUT THE AUTHOR

Paul Emerich France is a National Board Certified Teacher and consultant, dedicated to helping all learners feel seen, heard, and valued in the classroom. Paul writes for a number of prominent education publications, such as Educational Leadership, Edutopia, EdSurge, and the International Literacy Association's *Literacy Today*.

Paul has taught in multiple settings, ranging from transitional kindergarten to fifth grade. He has taught in both public and independent schools, even spending a bit of time in Silicon Valley, working for an education technology company, founding three microschools and building personalized learning software for the classroom. It was this experience that secured Paul's understanding of human-centered pedagogy that prioritizes humanity over technology.

Now, Paul is a sought-after writer and speaker, having presented at SXSW EDU and serving as keynote speaker at regional and national conferences. His teaching and thought leadership have been featured in the *Atlantic*, *WIRED*, and *The New Yorker*. Above all else, he enjoys connecting with his students and fellow teachers, encouraging all to have courageous conversations about identity to make learning personal for adults and children alike.

INTRODUCTION

WHY HUMANITY?

Humanization is not a novel concept. In fact, countless theorists before me have written about the idea of humanity in education, Paolo Freire being one of the most notable. To Freire, the process of humanization is one where we become more human as we age, grow, and learn (1970). This is not to imply that at any given point in time one is not human; this is, instead, intended to state that we begin our lives naked, unadulterated, and unconsciously human. It is our consciousness of our surroundings, ourselves, and our humanity that allows us to become even more human as we evolve.

Undoubtedly, we have come to a critical juncture in our history as a nation and as an increasingly globalized world. The world has been at the mercy of numerous pandemics in 2020. The first, of course, being the global coronavirus pandemic, threatening the health and safety of all of those who come in contact with it. The second being systemic racism, a centuries-long pandemic responsible for the marginalization, brutalization, and death of countless People of Color. The third, and less commonly spoken of pandemic being the threat of authoritarianism and fascism, mercilessly gripping American culture and countries around the world. The final being the impending and increasing threats that climate change has brought upon us, with the world very literally burning and waters visibly rising, threatening to swallow humanity whole should we neglect to act with expedience.

It would seem that humanity matters now more than ever, but I know that this is not true. Humanity has *always* mattered; it's just now that more and more of us with dominant identities are seeing just how dehumanizing American culture has been, and how dehumanized we've all been in the process.

I say this as a cisgender, homosexual white man—a person whose identity affords me insight into the experiences of both marginalized and dominant identities, who benefits from whiteness but is slighted by heteronormativity and the gender binary. As someone who identifies as gay, it has been easy for me to see how the LGBTQ+ community has been marginalized and dehumanized; but as a white man, it's only recently that Black leaders like Layla Saad, Ijeoma Oluo, Bettina Love, Ta-Nehisi Coates, and Ibram Kendi have opened my eyes to the degree to which white supremacy dominates our society, and to which it is responsible for the many pandemics we are experiencing now as a global society.

Our modern-day society, both in America and beyond, was built on dehumanization. Dating back to the earliest days of colonization, white people originating in Europe depended upon the oppression and marginalization of People of Color in order to expand their empires and bring wealth to their homelands (Kendi, 2019). They used brute force and violence to take control of people they saw as uncivilized and less than them, allowing the notion of white supremacy to guide their actions. Colonization has taken on many forms, from white people colonizing lands that did not belong to them, to the colonization of human beings, enslaving and exploiting them for free labor and exponential gains in wealth. American society grew within the colonialist mindset, expanding America's reach through Manifest Destiny, the inherent belief that white people were destined to control the land known as America, from "sea to shining sea." It continued into the Jim Crow era, where Black and Brown human beings were controlled and further colonized through unfair housing practices, segregation, and legislation that intended to assimilate Black and Brown students into white schools, as opposed to simply funding all schools equitably (Gladwell, 2017).

The practice of colonization continues into the present day, leading to crisis after crisis of which marginalized people—specifically working-class people and People of Color—bear the brunt. The 2008 financial crisis disproportionately impacted Black people, due to the fact that predatory mortgage lenders inflated the prices of housing, making it easy for people to default on their homes. This was similar to the unfair mortgage practices of the mid-20th century, where many Black buyers were forced to buy homes on contract, only to lose them if they missed even a single payment (Coates, 2014). Colonization shows up in lawmakers who seek to control the bodies of women and transgender people, pushing them to conform with the arbitrary norms of an aspiring theocracy. Colonization rears its ugly head within a health-care system that seeks to sink families into debt for getting sick and strives to trap young people into a lifetime's worth of payments in student loans, all to get an education that our society tells them they need to secure a job with decent pay.

Make no mistake, these practices that seek to control bodies and make human beings indebted to their societies are synonymous with those of indentured servitude. As victims of systems where human beings live within a never-ending cycle of debt, American citizens are, in fact, colonized by the ancestors of the same people who have committed and defended America's original sins.

Our minds, too, have been colonized—colonized by white supremacy (Saad, 2020) and patriarchal thinking, forcing us all to believe that this current reality in which we find ourselves and have been raised are the *right* ways, and that the collateral damage resulting from American capitalism—including systemic racism, climate change, and widening income inequality—are all just unfortunate byproducts of the way things have to be.

There is privilege in the statement "our humanity is at stake." There is privilege in that because if you are just now waking up to the idea that our humanity is at stake, you have been granted the privilege of living in a world where your humanity was not. Since I was old enough to realize that I was, in fact, a gay man and a member of the LGBTQ+ community, I came to terms with the idea that my psychological and physical safety was ephemeral. I've felt unsafe, unwelcome, and dehumanized in schools since the very beginning of my career, living in fear of being outed and ostracized by families and colleagues. I still live in that fear despite the fact that I make the choice every year to come out to my students. For People of Color, the reality of dehumanization is lifelong, realized from birth. In a country governed by white supremacy, the humanity of People of Color has always been at stake—and will be for quite some time, that is, until we rid our country of the forces that aim to further marginalize and stoke violence against People of Color.

So I'm not going to say that our humanity is at stake—because for so many of us, we have been stopped from fully realizing our humanity in the United States and in our schools, as a result of the oppressive policies that intend to keep cisgender, straight, white men in power. We have been limited in our ability to fully realize our humanity because of an aggrandized and unregulated form of free-market capitalism—American capitalism—that allows multibillionaires to amass tens of billions of dollars in the midst of a global pandemic and impending economic depression, while upward of 40 million Americans lost their jobs, struggling to make housing payments or put food on the table.

This is a book about teaching, and I do not mean to imply that changes in pedagogy are going to completely dismantle these systems that govern our everyday lives. But it is important to consider the sociopolitical context in which we find ourselves; it's important to examine the everyday classroom practices we take for granted through this economic lens, because classroom practices, too, have been colonized by white supremacy and the patriarchy, in hopes that by not examining them, we will deny ourselves the opportunity to imagine a different reality, one where each of us is able to step into our own humanity, and become all the more human as we grow and age.

Why humanization? No, it's not because our humanity is at stake. Our humanity has always been at stake, and our humanity likely will always be. We need to talk about humanization because it is the only answer. It is the only way that we can see through the chaos that these four pandemics have brought us and pave a path forward that gives us all a voice—that reaffirms all of our right to continuously actualize our humanity.

Bettina Love, author of *We Want to Do More Than Survive*, asked in a webinar in June of 2020 with Dena Simmons and Gholdy Muhammad through Haymarket Books, "Why did it take a pandemic to see the humanity in teaching?"

It's a good question. Why *did* it take a global crisis for parents and administrators alike to understand the role that teachers play in shaping the future of humanity in our country? And how did we lose sight of that so fast, in the few months that elapsed between the beginning of distance learning in March to the start of school in August and September, where so many teachers were given no choice or even the opportunity to provide input on how to return to school safely?

While the story may be long, the answer is quite simple: it's exceedingly clear that American society is dependent on the dehumanization of education, as well as its teachers and students. American society doesn't value teachers, teaching, and learning for anything more than its utilitarian purpose within the broader American economy—an economy that was built not only to reinforce white supremacy, but also to preserve the patriarchal oligarchy that governs every bit of our education system.

We have an opportunity here, as teachers, to use this moment in time as an opportunity for innovation, and above all else, that is what I hope to share with you over the course of this book. It is the silver lining—the stunning ring of light we can see while eclipsed by the darkness of this grave moment in time. Teachers across the country are grappling with how to adapt their pedagogy and make it suitable for online learning, and while I don't want to minimize the monumental nature of this task—to reimagine an entire classroom and curriculum virtually—I do want to encourage all teachers to center humanity and student liberation in the process of reimagining learning in the age of COVID-19.

In order to humanize teaching and learning, especially while having to teach and learn miles apart through screens, we must build independence within our students, so that they may become liberated learners and free thinkers who can encounter obstacles with persistence and learn how to learn; we must make collaboration and human connection essential components of our pedagogy, offering students the chance not only to socialize but to learn through collaboration with one another; we must center and unpack students' identities, helping them develop a conscious knowledge of themselves, all the while using their self-identified strengths to overcome their obstacles.

Over the course of this book, we'll explore all of these ideas as inputs to student liberation. In addition, we'll discuss what planning, preparing, and implementing humanized instruction looks like while teaching for student liberation—both digitally and in person. And finally, we'll explore technology integration, including the Digital Divide, which is no less than another manifestation of the compounding effects of systemic racism and inequity, as well as ways to minimize EdTech integration so that our collective sense of humanity can continue to be front and center.

It's ironic—or perhaps just a happy coincidence—that we are calling this style of pedagogy distance teaching. I wonder if, perhaps, it's the universe's way of challenging us. In some ways, shouldn't we always be teaching from a distance? In some ways, shouldn't we always be guiding students from the side, as opposed to hovering over them and dictating their every move?

No, this is not an endorsement of tech-centric learning, and this is not my way of advocating for us to always be learning from home. That said, I do see it as an opportunity for us to examine the problematic practices that we perpetuate while learning in person with our students, practices that enable dependent learning habits and industrialized models for curriculum consumption. I do see it as an opportunity for teachers to reflect on just how much we work against our collective goals for educational equity when we continue to enact these practices that are reminiscent of white supremacy and American capitalism.

But this is also not an indictment of the teachers who have been enacting these practices for quite some time. It's become clear that many school systems not only incentivize dehumanizing pedagogies, in some cases, they require them, holding teachers' jobs over their heads if they don't enact them.

The reality is that our humanity continues to be at stake, and that it will be for quite some time. The future may be unclear, the road may be rocky, and the story may continue to be long and winding as we push forward through this global crisis. But the answer will always be simple: We must teach and learn in pursuit of a deeper sense of collective humanity—and for no other reason.

CHAPTER ONE

TEACHING FOR LIBERATION

If one thing is clear, it's that the world is waking up to the fact that teachers do so much more than deliver content to their students. If not for parents having to experience firsthand what it's like to work with kids all day long, all the while teaching them important skills for the future, they may not have realized that teaching is more about socioemotional, executive functioning skills, and independent learning habits than it is about academic content.

Our primary goal should always be to foster independence in our students, for independence guides students toward their own liberation. In *Culturally Responsive Teaching and the Brain*, Zaretta Hammond (2014) writes about the difference between independent and dependent learners within classrooms. Dependent learners rely on adults or technology in order to acquire academic content, while independent learners think critically, ask questions, and draw from a toolbox of strategies in order to learn with a healthy amount of independence, setting them up for a lifetime of learning.

That's not to conflate independence with individualism. In *Dismantling Racism: A Workbook for Social Change Groups*, co-authors Kenneth Jones and Tema Okun (2001) identify fourteen characteristics of white supremacy culture, including the following:

- Perfectionism
- Sense of Urgency
- Defensiveness
- Quantity Over Quality
- Worship of the Written Word
- Paternalism
- Either/Or Thinking
- Power Hoarding
- Fear of Open Conflict
- Individualism
- Progress Is Bigger, More
- Objectivity
- Right to Comfort
- Only One Right Way

White supremacy is a system of oppression based on the inherent belief that white people are superior to People of Color (Saad, 2020). Such beliefs systems were used to justify enslavement, subjugation, and separation of Black people across generations of American history. While slavery as an institution was abolished in the 19th century, it's vestiges still permeate most of our contemporary institutions. Every American, regardless of individual political leanings, embodies aspects of white supremacy. Most of us can identify with perfectionism and the deep sense of shame that comes from making mistakes, or the sense of urgency we all feel to get things done as efficiently as possible, to not waste any time or money in the process.

It's important to recognize that an overemphasis on individualism is symptomatic of white supremacist thinking, too, so I don't want to—even for a moment—imply that students should only be working on their own while learning from a distance. That's not what independent learning means. In fact, it's quite the opposite. Our goals for learning should be to deepen students' individual senses of humanity, as well as our collective sense of it. As a result, we should be maximizing time for students to collaborate with peers and otherwise learn from and within the collective classroom community. Independence, in the context of this book, really means that students should not become overreliant on their teachers, parents, or peers to problem-solve, but they should, by all means, be empowered to leverage their community for learning.

Challenges with independence occur frequently with "high performing" students who are readily able to play by the rules of school. These students perform well on standardized assessments and otherwise keep up with the compliance metrics of school, only to crumble when faced with an open-ended question, unexpected obstacle, or uncertain situation that requires them to think on their feet. But we also know that independent learning is especially challenging for students who have historically struggled in school. More often than not, teachers and parents alike too often employ practices that perpetuate dependence when working with struggling students. While the intentions are good, they tend to over scaffold their teaching for struggling learners, creating a maladaptive pattern where students believe they need a teacher to read the directions to them, organize their work, or otherwise provide scaffolds that are neither least restrictive nor in the best interest of student liberation. This maladaptive tendency assumes the worst in struggling students, undoubtedly contributing to a subconscious self-perception that is disempowering, compounding upon itself with each subtle message that they can't learn without assistance.

Because we no longer have the consistent luxury of teaching and learning within close physical proximity to our students, teachers across the country are reckoning with their practice. It's becoming exceedingly clear that too many teachers are employing teaching strategies that unintentionally promote dependence in the classroom. These strategies rely on compliance metrics and control-based tactics that not only get us farther away from our collective goals for student liberation; these strategies also oppress students, creating barriers for Students of Color, LGBTQ+ students, and neurodivergent students. Distance learning has only made the negative effects of these practices more pronounced, because it's not possible to hover over a child and dictate their every move while teaching through a screen. This is part of the reason why distance learning has challenged so many educators: We have grown accustomed to hovering over our students, in an attempt to guarantee success, appease parents, and prevent students from failing.

In her book, Hammond (2014) also shares that the students who most need tools for independent learning are often the least likely to get them. Make no mistake, this is not because teachers do not want to provide them with these tools; it is because a majority of the school systems that serve Black and Brown students are not invested in providing tools that help students liberate themselves and dismantle white supremacy. Instead, schools that serve predominantly Black and Brown students are dependent on test scores that either show satisfactory "achievement" or "growth." This is true for neurodivergent students, as well.

This emphasis on test scores ultimately incentivizes administrators and teachers alike to take the most efficient path to the highest quantitative gains, resulting in teaching tactics that make students receptacles for grade-level content, as opposed to critical and conscious constructors of knowledge within classrooms.

So how do we build independence while teaching from a distance? Better yet, how do we help teachers detach from these archaic practices and move toward student liberation?

Learning is an artful blend of consumption and creation—and we must help our students find this balance. All learning should be a conversation and an exchange, one that requires learners to take in new information, meanwhile applying it to novel contexts, perhaps even creating novel ideas or works as a result of their learning. When we teach in a manner that emphasizes rote memorization or content consumption, we rob our students of this exchange of ideas. Learning becomes a one-way street—purely consumptive and mindless. We neither want one nor the other, at least in their entirety. We want students to both critically and consciously toggle between creation and consumption.

Students who only consume in the classroom do so passively and mindlessly in response to extrinsic motivators like grades, acceptance to elite universities, a satisfying career, and promises of a lavish lifestyle. Overly didactic teaching methods that value lecture-based teaching or rote memorization make students consumers of academic content, forcing them to take in information and regurgitate it on a test. Moreover, we have ample evidence that students with access to wealth and privilege perform best in such systems, in that they have access to a range of supplemental supports such as tutoring. Conversely, creation is not possible without consumption. In order to create something new, students must consume ideas or materials in the process. This is not to say that consuming to create is necessarily bad. Instead, what's most desirable is striking a balance between the two—responsibly and sustainably consuming content to create new ideas, make novel connections, and solve real problems. In fact, the notion of creating without consuming feels isolated, siloed, and disembodied from the surrounding world.

We know we're doing something right when students strike a balance between creation and consumption in our classrooms. Why? Because we know that they're using the knowledge and skills from our lessons and applying them to their projects or assignments. We know that they're learning how to learn. In a way, this requires always teaching from a distance, per se, so we can give our students space to take risks, make mistakes, and cultivate the necessary learning habits to stand on their own, striking a balance between mindfully consuming and consciously creating.

LEARNING HOW TO LEARN

Most educators would agree that in an age when information is available with a single click, learning how to learn matters far more than the acquisition of content. While we can reasonably assume that many of the academic skills we teach students will be applicable and valuable to their futures, the fact of the matter is that the students who learn in our classrooms right now will live vastly different lives than their teachers do, tasked with solving problems we never imagined and required to fill jobs we never dreamed possible.

Many like to emphasize these *jobs* that our students will have and how creating lifelong learners will set students up for success in whatever jobs they may have when they're older. And while it's true that our students will, of course, need to find jobs in adulthood, I think about it a bit differently.

Our students will inherit our challenges. They will be faced with some of the greatest obstacles that humanity has ever faced. We need our students to grow into critical thinkers and creative problem solvers that will approach challenges with hope and resilience, so they can pick up where we left off in combatting climate change, systemic racism, and the economic inequality that has resulted from unregulated capitalism.

If we know that the students we teach will need to be prepared for this future, we must strike a balance between explicitly teaching core skills and helping them learn how to learn. We need to cultivate within our students an **awareness** of the learning process; the ability to **advocate** for themselves while learning; the capacity to **reflect** on their successes and challenges while learning; and finally, the conviction to **act** so that they may build resilience and continuously engage in productive learning experiences.

SELF-AWARENESS

Independence and self-awareness go hand-in-hand, and I would go so far as to argue that self-awareness is an antecedent to all productive independent learning experiences. After all, if you're not aware of what's happening in your mind, your body, and your heart, how can you possibly take a confident step in the right direction?

"I don't get it," Anwar said to me, a phrase I've heard many times before.

"What do you mean?" I asked.

"I'm just stuck," he said yet again.

"Well, let's start with rereading the problem," I said, pointing to the task in his math journal.

Anwar read the math task aloud to me. You'd be surprised how many times a simple read-aloud of a task's directions solves their problem. It's not uncommon for students to erupt with realization after having actually read the problem closely. Imagine that.

But this wasn't the case for Anwar. Rereading the problem didn't help him overcome his obstacle. He remained stuck, unaware of what step to take and in which direction he wanted to go.

"It's hard for me to help you when I don't know exactly what's getting you stuck," I replied to him. This wasn't just a tactic for helping him become more aware of what his obstacle was. It was also just the truth. It is, in fact, very challenging to help our students when we cannot identify the root cause of their misunderstanding. In my opinion, our best bet for *truly* helping our students—and not just putting a band-aid on their problems—is cultivating awareness around their obstacles and helping them articulate what, precisely, it is that they "don't get."

I honored wait time as best I could, but deafening silence ensued. Truly, I was baffled.

"Here's something I do," I replied. "Sometimes when I don't understand the problem, I try to draw it first."

It seemed relatively straight forward to me. It was a simple multiplication problem: one that could be solved in a variety of ways. I was most certainly tempted to simply show him a method and leave it at that, but I always think about the long-term implications of even the simplest actions in the classroom. By doing it for him, I was serving myself. By challenging him to identify his obstacle on his own, I was serving him and helping him discover a strategy for liberated learning, one that he could use even when I wasn't right next to him.

"I'll be back in a few minutes," I said. I left his side and circulated around the classroom until I came back to him just a few minutes later.

Much to my surprise, he had actually represented the problem accurately. He drew pictures of the donuts and the boxes they'd be in. He clearly could see the problem was looking for the total number of donuts.

"How's it going?" I queried. He looked up at me forlornly.

"I still don't get it," he replied, looking down at his math journal. "I'm not sure what this word means."

He pointed to the word *product*. What is the *product* of the donuts in all boxes?

"Excellent work!" I exclaimed. "You figured out what you didn't understand. It was the word "product." Do you have any idea what you think it might mean?"

He looked at me blankly.

"Sometimes mathematicians have to make *assumptions*. Sometimes they have to *infer* when they are not sure. Could you make an educated guess?"

He thought for a moment. "Maybe the total number of donuts from all the boxes?"

"Exactly," I said. "The product is basically just the answer for a multiplication question. It's the total number after multiplying."

Anwar started working on his math journal, relief lifting his shoulders and changing his entire mood.

"Let's stop and reflect on this moment," I said to him. "What got you stuck?"

"That word," he said. "Product."

"Exactly," I replied. "And what might you do differently to be more independent next time?"

"Maybe make a guess about the word?"

"Sure," I affirmed, "you could make a guess. But you could also *infer* based on what you see in the problem, and you could always ask a tablemate if you need a word clarified, too."

Being independent doesn't necessarily mean doing things entirely on your own; instead, being independent entails being aware of what you know, what you don't, and what you need in order to overcome obstacles. For Anwar, it all came down to one word, and while I likely hadn't solved all of his problems with dependent learning, the next time he came to something he "didn't get," I'd be able to remind him of this moment, where all he needed to do was a bit of inferring.

SELF-ADVOCACY

Self-regulation is powerful. So is dysregulation. Self-regulation oftentimes provides a clear path to independence, while dysregulation frequently shuts down independent learning. For this reason, self-regulation can be one of the most powerful tools to help students learn independently.

But we must be incredibly conscious of how we leverage self-regulation skills in the classroom. Social and emotional learning (SEL) can be weaponized against Black and Brown students, students living in poverty, and LGBTQ+ students. The National Equity Project (2020) provides a handful of culturally responsive recommendations for teaching social and emotional skills on their website, including but not limited to approaching SEL work with the "explicitly stated purpose of creating more equitable learning environments and outcomes," as well as using SEL to "facilitate healing from the effects of systemic oppression, build cross-racial alliances, and create joyful, liberatory learning environments." This means that if we are encouraging students to self-regulate, we must be sure we're encouraging them to use self-regulation as a tool for self-liberation through self-advocacy, and not as a means for compliance, tone policing, or control.

"You seem really angry," I said to one of my students one day, noticing her squinted eyes and lack of eye contact.

Immediately after I said it, I realized the potential impact of what I was saying. Here I was, a white man, telling a Black female student that she seemed angry. While people of all genders and races can experience anger, I became astutely aware of the power dynamic at play here. I was dangerously close to reinforcing the stereotype of the "angry Black girl" if I didn't exercise my own self-regulation.

"I am," she replied, looking down at the table. I was relieved that, at the very least, I read her correctly. But I was a bit worried about what was coming next.

"Will you talk to me about it?" I asked.

"Well," she confided in me, "I just feel like you are always helping me. And sometimes I don't need help."

I stopped, I breathed, and I listened.

"I wasn't ready for help today," she said. "I was just sitting at my desk thinking, and I wasn't confused. You do that a lot."

My heart sank. Here I was, just trying to help, and all the while, I was doing harm.

Intention rarely matters as much as impact does, and it was clear that my impact here was overwhelmingly negative. By hovering and intervening too soon, I was working against equity in my classroom. I was reinforcing *dependent* learning habits, as opposed to the independence I so coveted. Worst of all, I was acting in opposition to this student's liberation. Could it possibly have been due to my own internalized racial biases? Perhaps. Did I want to change it? You bet I did.

Oftentimes, when white people are called out—or in this case, called in—to their biases, we respond with defensiveness. Recall that defensiveness is, in fact, a characteristic of white supremacy. We *must* exercise self-restraint in moments like these. When our students are courageous enough to advocate for themselves in these moments, they are offering us a moment to learn, not only about themselves, but about our own teaching, as well. While it makes me uncomfortable to admit the possibility that my actions were grounded in unconscious racial bias, it's entirely possible—and dare I say, even likely—that they were. But what mattered most was the way my actions made that student feel. Countless other students in that same situation likely would not have advocated for themselves in that way. I was grateful she did because it gave me a gift that I certainly didn't earn. She gave me the gift of critical feedback, a check on my bias, and a reminder that if I exercise more self-regulation and teach more from a distance, my students might surprise me with how independent they actually can be.

SELF-REFLECTION

None of these matter without reflection. John Hattie, award winning educator and best-selling author, tells us that self-reported grades and self-reflection have significant impacts on student learning (Hattie, 2017). In fact, they are seen as some of the highest impact strategies that one can use in the classroom, and it makes sense why: self-reporting grades requires a great deal of self-reflection, and self-reflection requires sophisticated self-awareness and a clear articulation of learning goals, strengths, and challenges. In essence, by building self-reflection skills, we are helping students identify what they've already learned and what they need to learn, aiding the process of learning how to learn.

You'll notice in Anwar's story, I made a point to stop him, even though he was suddenly "unstuck."

"Let's stop and reflect on this moment," I said.

I did this for a very specific reason. While it's possible that Anwar might not have made the same mistake the next time around, it's also highly possible that he would have, had I neglected to cultivate awareness around the source of his obstacle. Taking the brief moment to reflect reduces the likelihood of having to address the same issue multiple times.

When teaching from a distance, we must constantly rely on self-reflection in order to help students grow their independence in the learning process. While moments like these of interpersonal and informal reflection can happen at innumerous times throughout the day, they also can happen more formally, albeit less frequently.

I offer a rather simple template for reflection, because oftentimes, reflection is really that simple. When reflecting, we want students to operate from a strengths-based mindset, first and foremost able to see the positive aspects of their work, and we want them to use those strengths to overcome any challenges or obstacles related to their work. As a result, in conjunction with feedback I provide after formative or summative assessments, I also provide a reflection sheet that allows students to put their strengths and challenges into their own words, using my written feedback as potential material to include in their reflection. Not only does this build independent learning habits, articulating their reflections in writing grants them the opportunity of practicing this critical skill before they share their work with their parents. That way, when parents ask "how they did" on a given assessment or project, they are equipped to discuss their strengths, their challenges, and their next action steps. While sometimes I use a strengths and challenges T-chart to structure reflection, other times I scaffold this by using Project Zero's "I used to . . . Now I . . ." thinking routine, as well as a listing structure for action steps.

With enough repetition, self-reflection becomes an integral part of our classroom culture. As we'll discuss in the next chapter, student liberation is supported by a classroom culture that values self-reflection. Eventually, students begin reflecting without the activity you see in Figure 1.1. They may even do it without prompting from me. This is critical to independent learning and liberating students from dependence on a teacher. When they can reflect on their own, they can initiate improvements to their own work, allowing them to learn on their own.

Figure 1.1: Distance Learning Reflection Template

Reflection	Celebrations
I used to . . .	Now I . . .

My Action Steps

- _____
  _____
- _____
  _____
- _____
  _____

TAKING ACTION

Self-awareness, self-advocacy, and self-reflection are useless if they don't result in a change in behavior. That is why moving our students to action is critical to learning how to learn and building effective learning habits.

"I'm just feeling really confused," I said to Monroe.

"Why?" he replied.

"Well, I notice that you keep using the stacking method for subtraction, and most of the time, you get an answer that doesn't really make sense. Do you remember having this conversation last time?"

Monroe nodded in accord.

I see this a lot, especially at the beginning of a school year. Students come into the classroom trying to replicate algorithms or strategies they see their older siblings or parents using. In some cases, parents teach their children these unknowingly complex algorithms for computation with good intention, thinking they are helping them get ahead or master an essential skill. But this works against students when they execute them incorrectly or don't have the number sense to evaluate the accuracy of their answer.

"Do you remember the strategy you used last time?" I asked Monroe.

"The open number line?" he said.

"Yes," I replied. "The open number line. Do you remember how to use that?"

He said he did, and so I asked him to try that strategy on his own while I went and helped one of his tablemates. When I came back a few minutes later, Monroe had successfully found the difference between two three-digit numbers using an open number line.

"Wow," I said, "it looks like this strategy worked really well for you this time. What do you think?"

Monroe agreed. The strategy worked, and not only that, it was an easy tool to use.

"Will you write down a quick reflection for me in your math journal?" I asked him. "Will you write down 'I used to use stacking to subtract, but now I . . . '"

"Use open number lines!" he finished my sentence.

"That's right," I said, "and I want that to be your action step for the next time. I want you to think of this moment, and I want you to remember that open number lines are a reliable strategy for you. You almost always get the right answer when you use them. Will you write that down, too? Will you write 'Next time, I will . . . '"

Monroe filled in the rest of the sentence. *Next time, I will use open number lines to subtract because they work better for me.* While it was not a guarantee that Monroe would remember to use open number lines, identifying the action step made it more likely, bringing us back to building his self-awareness through identifying an action step.

LEVERAGING CONFERENCES FOR HABITS CHECK-INS

You'll notice that most of the stories I tell take place in these moments when I'm providing individualized feedback to students. That's because this sort of interpersonal feedback is truly what powers learning in our classrooms. These moments where we can provide honest, specific, timely, and action-able feedback for our students are the greatest gifts we can give them. These moments reveal our true purpose in the classroom. It's not necessarily to be an all-knowing influence, dishing out knowledge and "correct answers" all the time; it is, instead, to be guides for our students, assisting them in identifying strategies that help them learn on their own.

This is critical in distance learning, and my hope is that by shifting to a focus on learning habits, your in-person pedagogy will allow you to teach at a healthy distance, as well. When students are learning virtually, we don't have the luxury of circulating and assisting them with every obstacle or unexpected challenge. They need to have tools and strategies for overcoming them on their own. They must be self-aware and able to articulate the root cause of their obstacles, able to advocate for themselves, ready to reflect honestly on their strengths and challenges, and empowered to take action, initiating changes to their work or their learning habits.

Ultimately, these conferences and the feedback within them provide students with the keys to liberate themselves—not necessarily providing us with the keys to liberate *them*. While there are pedagogies and tools that are unique to what I hope is a temporary phase of digitally dependent distance learning, building effective learning habits is critical to liberated learning no matter where students are—whether they are in person next to us or interacting with us through their screens. I've started our conversation about distance learning here, because by centering student independence, we not only liberate our students from archaic practices that require us to hover over and micromanage students, we also liberate ourselves from the compounding workload that stems from micromanaging our students.

TIPS FOR TEACHING FROM A DISTANCE, CHAPTER 1

- Prioritize learning how to learn over content acquisition.

- Cultivate self-awareness in students by challenging them to identify their obstacles.

- Encourage students to advocate for themselves.

- Check yourself on your biases and examine how your unconscious bias might be causing you to assist students when they don't need it.

- Make self-reflection a part of your daily practice.

- Use formal, written self-reflection as a part of your assessment routine.

- Encourage students to identify action steps that help them change maladaptive strategies or learning habits.

- Leverage conferences to provide feedback on learning habits, in addition to misconceptions with content.

CHAPTER TWO

INTENSIFYING SOCIOEMOTIONAL LEARNING

Academics matter, and I would even go so far to say that academics should be a major component of distance learning. I bond with my kids over learning, as all teachers do. I connect with them over good books, the stories they write, and challenging math problems. But we also must recognize that our students have endured what will become the generational trauma of a global pandemic. Our students will bring big feelings, real worries, and valid fears into our classrooms as a result of the pandemic.

Experiencing a global pandemic has been traumatic for all of us, and as educators, we cannot take this lightly. The education world is waking up to the effects of trauma on students, and as a result, educators should be decentering academics, intensifying socioemotional work, and finding ways to incorporate trauma-informed practices into their everyday pedagogy.

But it's important to note that understanding trauma-informed teaching is not only important because we are living through the COVID pandemic. Black and Brown students, LGBTQ+ students, and neurodivergent students wake up in a world that more frequently feels unsafe; they venture out into a society that was not built for them. To my white readers, I urge you to remember that our nation experienced more than one pandemic in 2020. For Black and Brown people, white supremacy is a centuries-long pandemic, the result of which is a profound generational trauma that has been burned into the DNA of every Black and Brown student who enters our classrooms (DeGruy, 2005). LGBTQ+ students are constantly faced with the traumatic impacts of homophobic and transphobic microaggressions, and students with disabilities and/or neurodivergent students are served repeated reminders that their way of interacting with the world is often considered second, needing to be accommodated instead of centered. The COVID-19 pandemic has likely exacerbated trauma for all of these groups.

To add insult to injury, social and emotional learning teaching strategies have been weaponized against Students of Color, LGBTQ+ students, and neurodivergent students.

Dena Simmons, author and assistant director of the Yale Center for Emotional Intelligence, described socioemotional learning as "white supremacy with a hug," if not taught in tandem with explicit anti-racist and anti-bias practices (Madda, 2019). While self-regulation is a critical component of socio-emotional learning, as defined by the Collaborative for Academic, Social, and Emotional Learning (CASEL), encouraging self-regulation can easily become a means for the control and further oppression of marginalized students.

In her *New York Times* bestselling book, *So You Want to Talk About Race*, Ijeoma Oluo (2018) defines "tone policing" as a person of privilege not necessarily pushing back against *what* is being said, but instead the *way* it is being discussed. Tone policing and the weaponization of self-regulation go hand in hand, and in order to take a trauma-informed approach in an era of distance learning, we must understand that sometimes our students' communication of their "big" feelings will mirror the feelings themselves. When students feel sad, we will likely see sadness in their eyes, and when they feel the pang of anger that results from the stings of injustice, we will likely see anger in their bodies and hear it in their voices. This has to be expected; this has to be okay. We can't possibly convince our students that we're interested in building a safe place to express feelings, all the while policing the manner in which they're communicating. To be liberated means to be able to share feelings openly, without judgment or repercussion.

When teaching from a distance, we must be more sensitive than we have ever been to the trauma our students bring into our classrooms on a daily basis. We must be aware that trauma is not confined to the global pandemic in which we've all found ourselves; it is ever present, intertwined with our students' and their families' identities. The challenge in our digital classrooms is that we no longer have the benefit of reading body language and facial expressions to the degree we could before. We must, instead, build new structures into our classrooms that center socioemotional literacy and ensure our students that we are still here to provide them with emotional support—and we must remember to keep these structures in place even long after distance learning is no longer a part of our reality.

In "A Trauma-Informed Approach to Teaching Through Coronavirus," the Teaching Tolerance Staff encourages educators to consider three key areas that are often disrupted in times of trauma: sense of safety, connectedness, and hope (2020). Consider some of the following tools, strategies, and structures to fortify your classroom culture with safety, connectedness, and hope.

STRUCTURE IS HEALING

I can't stress enough the importance of structure in classrooms. My husband, who works as a licensed clinical social worker in Chicago, always says that "chaos is trauma and structure is healing." To be trauma-informed means to provide structure, reliability, and continuity for kids in the midst of this traumatic chaos.

Our commitment to providing children the structure that they need is not because their parents are unable to give it to them. Yet it goes without saying that, as teachers, this is something we can provide that is far more meaningful than literacy or mathematics instruction. While our students may not want to admit it, many of them love the routine of school. They love knowing what to expect, and they find a sense of safety and comfort in reliably predicting what's coming.

Structure always starts with the schedule. When my school transitioned to distance learning, I created visual schedules for my students, with a checklist of expected activities (see Figure 2.1 on the next page). On the checklist, I also included their specials classes and a reminder to log in if it was a synchronous class.

The regularity of our schedule from the Spring served my students and me well. They knew I'd be available every morning at 8:00 a.m., in case they needed something, or in the event that I needed to work with them a bit more. They knew that we'd begin the day with a brief morning meeting and reading workshop, take a break, and meet back for synchronous math workshop at 11:00 a.m. They came to expect a final meeting at 1:00 p.m. for writing workshop. Our classes also followed a relatively similar structure. Because my learning blocks were already structured off of derivatives of the workshop model, which we'll address in Chapter 7, my students knew that we'd come together for a minilesson, spend time working in small groups and conferencing, and then reconvene at the end of the learning block for a reflection.

I knew this schedule and the cadence of my learning blocks provided the structure I intended because when I inevitably spent too long conferencing or working with small groups, I'd receive a message in Google Hangouts: "Hi, Mr. France, don't we have to come back to the whole-group Meet for reflection?"

Schedule
Week of 4/6/2020

	Monday 4/6	Tuesday 4/7	Wednesday 4/8	Thursday 4/9	Friday 4/10
8.00	Make sure you are able to log into **Meet** and that you can see the upcoming meeting. **If you can't, contact Mr. France and Miss Gannon.**	**Specials** ☐ Computer Science Activity Card ☐ Spanish Activity Card	**Office Hours** ☐ Practice logging in for office hours	**Office Hours** ☐ Art Activity Card	NO SCHOOL
9.00	**Reading Workshop** ☐ Reading Log ☐ Seesaw Card ☐ Practice using Hangouts with Mr. France	**Reading Workshop** ☐ Reading Log ☐ Seesaw Card	**Reading Workshop** ☐ Reading Log ☐ Seesaw Card	**Reading Workshop** ☐ Reading Log ☐ Seesaw Card	NO SCHOOL
10.00	**BREAK**	**Specials** ☐ Library Activity Card	**Music** ☐ Log in for class	**Science** ☐ Log in for class	NO SCHOOL
11.00	**Math Workshop** ☐ Anchor Task ☐ Workbook Pages ☐ Document on Seesaw Card	**Math Workshop** ☐ Anchor Task ☐ Workbook Pages ☐ Document on Seesaw Card	**Math Workshop** ☐ Anchor Task ☐ Workbook Pages ☐ Document on Seesaw Card	**Math Workshop** ☐ Anchor Task ☐ Workbook Pages ☐ Document on Seesaw Card	NO SCHOOL
12.00	**LUNCH**	**LUNCH**	**LUNCH**	**LUNCH**	NO SCHOOL
1.00	**Writing Workshop** ☐ Set a Daily Goal ☐ Document Progress on Seesaw Card	**Writing Workshop** ☐ Set a Daily Goal ☐ Document Progress on Seesaw Card	**Writing Workshop** ☐ Set a Daily Goal ☐ Document Progress on Seesaw Card	**Writing Workshop** ☐ Set a Daily Goal ☐ Document Progress on Seesaw Card	NO SCHOOL
2.00	**Specials** ☐ PE Activity	**Specials** ☐ PE Activity	**Specials** ☐ PE Activity	**Specials** ☐ PE Activity	NO SCHOOL

24

"We do!" I'd say in reply. "Thanks for reminding me."

Kids derive structure not only from the predictability of a schedule, they also find the healing nature of structure when classroom agreements are upheld, and when adults set clear boundaries for behavior.

Liam had struggled most of the year with behavior in the classroom. Without revealing too much about his learning profile, I can say that physical regulation challenged him and that he historically had struggled with attention and focus. He also required a great deal of validation. He'd frequently ask me questions that I knew he could answer on his own. I saw beyond this behavior within the first weeks of school and partnered with parents to develop a plan for helping him become more independent, weaning him off of the constant counterproductive validation he seemed to be seeking from me.

It was clear that distance learning was a struggle for him. While he was always present in our synchronous learning sessions and giving his best effort to participate, I could see through his camera that he was reeling. Within his tiny box of my computer screen, I could see that he was always in motion, and frequently I'd have to remind him to mute his microphone, as he'd not realize it was on, sending ancillary sounds echoing into the speakers of the remaining twenty students.

When a child violates classroom agreements, it should not be a means for punishment. Instead, it's an indicator that we need to get to the root of the problem. After reaching out to Liam's parents, getting some more information on what was challenging for him, and doing some reflecting on what was and was not working with my distance learning practices, I scheduled a conversation with Liam to chat some more.

"I'm just really tired," he said. "It's hard to stare at a screen all day."

"I understand," I replied. "It *is* really hard."

"And I have all of this work that I haven't finished from my other classes," he said, referring to art, music, and other specials. "I feel like I have so much to do, and then I can't finish up my work for reading and writing and math, too."

It became clear to me through listening to Liam that he needed a lighter workload. He was unable to cope with its demands, given the fact that his learning profile already necessitated modifications. It became clear that Liam needed all of his teachers (including his interventionist and the specials teachers) to collaborate on a plan that would reduce his workload and his anxiety. It was also clear that Liam needed an extra outlet—a time to check in and talk about his feelings, his workload, and to clarify things from our synchronous sessions that were confusing or unclear.

"Liam," I said, "how would you feel about setting up a time in your calendar every day where we can check in and talk? I can help you finish assignments, clarify things from class, or even just check in to see how things are going. Would that help?"

Liam jumped at the opportunity for a little extra one-on-one time, adding structure and safety to his schedule that I'm certain helped ease some of his anxiety for the duration of the school year. Each day, shortly after our 9:00 morning session, Liam and I would check in. Some days, it wasn't necessary, and Liam elected to go to his synchronous special instead of chatting with me. Other days, it *was* necessary. While it didn't alleviate every challenge that Liam encountered, it provided a support that was appropriate and helped him cope with the chaos, uncertainty, and challenges of distance learning. I couldn't help but wonder: Why didn't I do this more during the school year? Why couldn't I build this structure into my classroom more regularly?

I won't be too hard on myself. There were, in fact, times where I checked in with kids one on one to see how they were coping with friendship challenges, changes to their family structure, or even in an effort to provide some extra academic help, but making it a regular part of the school day once we return back to in-person learning could, without a doubt, drastically change our students' experiences and counterintuitively make them more independent in their learning.

But wait, how could *more* support and *more* one-on-one time actually *help* with independence in the classroom?

I can't help but think it's because of trust. When our students know we are there to build trust with them, support them, and help them pick themselves up when they've fallen down, they are more apt to take risks, make mistakes, and otherwise stand on their own. They learn quickly that falling down doesn't mean they've done something wrong or that their teacher will be upset with them; they learn that teachers who check in on them care about them. They feel safe because they feel supported, they feel important, and they feel *connected* to the adult they see each and every day—even if it's through a computer screen.

A SENSE OF COMMUNITY

At the beginning of each synchronous learning block, I made a conscious choice to start with an emotional check-in. My students had grown accustomed to using Leah Kuypers's *Zones of Regulation* vernacular (2011), and as a result, my kids would start each learning block by sharing which zone they were in, if they were comfortable. I did, too, as a way to continue modeling what it looked like to share the wide range of feelings that we humans experience on a day-to-day basis. Some days, I was tired, and I told them. Truth be told, they could probably see it, too. Other days, I was optimistic and excited to work on their projects with them. And some days, I was angry. I was angry that the world felt like it was on fire or frustrated that one of our digital tools was malfunctioning, throwing a wrench into my plans for the day. We're often conditioned to believe that these negative feelings are counterproductive to a healthy and happy classroom culture, but I assure you they are not. When we don't model how we deal with uncomfortable feelings like anger or sadness, we send an implicit message that there's something wrong with us when we experience these emotions. When we model how to communicate "big" feelings, we normalize them, helping students learn how to communicate them effectively, too.

In order to give every child a chance to share, I leveraged the chat function in Google Meet. While some students shared by unmuting and describing their emotional state in greater depth, others shared succinctly with an emoji that corresponded with the color of the zone in which they found themselves. Red stop signs meant they were dysregulated or upset, while green shamrocks showed they were feeling ready to learn.

Naturally, when coming to a synchronous learning session, some students were early, while others were late. Talking about our feelings was the perfect way to keep them productively occupied while we waited for the remaining students to join us. For my latecomers, the conversation was easy to join, partially because we did the emotional check-ins so frequently, but also because it required no prerequisite knowledge. It simply required showing up and being human.

Stretching and deep breathing has been proven to lower stress and anxiety in students, and as a result, we coupled our emotional check-ins with a stretching routine led by my co-teacher, Logan. Luckily for me, Logan had a second job as a yoga teacher, and so leading the students in a recurring yoga practice was right up her alley. That said, you don't need to be a yoga teacher to lead your students in stretching and breathing. In fact, we drew from a couple of very simple, child-friendly poses, including child's pose, cat-cow, downward-facing dog, and mountain pose. With enough structure and routine, students began to volunteer to lead our stretches, deepening their connection not only to the routine, but to each other. Kids love to learn from one another; they love to be leaders and to do the things their teachers do. Leading our stretching exercises allowed them to do that.

These stretching routines and our emotional check-ins not only created a predictable cadence to our asynchronous sessions, they provided students with a sense of community, too. Stretching and yoga became a part of our classroom culture, and our emotional check-ins served as a tool for connecting with each other and showing that we cared for one another's well-being.

Connectedness doesn't only have to entail socioemotional learning. As I mentioned earlier, I bond with my students over the core subjects and academics, and students can bond with each other over academic learning in the classroom, too.

In Chapter 7, we'll discuss small-group instruction, but in this chapter, we'll only examine small-group and collaborative learning in the context of socioemotional learning, trauma-informed instruction, and building a sense of community.

One of the most salient arguments in favor of returning to in-person learning is the social isolationism that has inevitably resulted from distance learning and a global pandemic.

"I feel it, too," I would say to the kids. "I miss my friends, too. You are not alone."

I'm sure that these words of reassurance did little to actually make them feel better, but I also gently reminded them of the reality that being in person simply wasn't safe right now. The likelihood for so many of us, for that matter, is that if we contracted COVID-19, we'd likely be fine. But it's also possible that we wouldn't be—or that someone we love or a vulnerable person with an underlying condition wouldn't be either. It's not only up to us to recognize these truths in times of crisis, as adults; it's up to us to build empathic capital in our students during these tender times. We must help them see that their actions could, in fact, have ripple effects—in the case of the COVID pandemic, that by going out in public without a mask or going on playdates could make the pandemic worse and impact people who lack the health privilege that they have.

While socialization may look different in the COVID era, using a disproportionate amount of time to engage students in small-group and collaborative learning experiences mitigates social isolationism and provides students with at least some of the social interaction that they need. I was pleasantly surprised with my third-grade class in the Spring of 2020 when they engaged in Research Clubs, a Unit of Study in the Lucy Calkins Reading Workshop Curriculum (2015). While small groups can be easily achieved through Break Out Groups, I ended up using separate Google Meet rooms that I could jump in and out of with ease, checking in on group dynamics and the progress they were making on their research. I even spent a handful of lunch hours with a Google Meet open, allowing my students to talk freely and socialize while I muted my microphone and turned off my camera. In talking with a group of kindergarten teachers toward the end of the year, they shared that they had a specified time of day called "table talks," where kindergarten students would set up their iPads on the floor or a table and engage in free play while they simply talked to their friends, getting much needed social interaction, albeit in a vastly different format.

It's not lost on me that social connection and a sense of community matter. Especially in the midst of a global pandemic where so many of us are confined to our homes, our kids need to socialize. It's a critical part of learning. But there are, in fact, ways to make this happen from the safety and comfort of our own homes—especially if doing so means saving lives in times of crisis. We just need to be creative about it.

HOPE AND GRATITUDE

We couldn't have been but a few days into distance learning before my students began asking a number of questions, none of which I felt I could answer:

- What about the musical at the end of the year? Will that still be happening?

- How are the Olympics going to work this year? Will we still have them?

- When are we going back, Mr. France? Are we *ever* going back?

The fact was that I just didn't know. And I didn't know how to tell them that I didn't know. I didn't always know how to say that I was scared, that I was grieving the loss of all of these things, and that I had absolutely no idea, when—or if—we'd be back in school together again.

Teaching Tolerance (www.tolerance.org) provides a handful of recommendations for helping students find hope in times of trauma or crisis. This includes talking about historical times of crisis, going outside and getting some fresh air, and even sharing stories of positive affirmations and hope. All of these things are helpful to do when trying to instill a sense of hope in your students. In addition to these, I recommend a daily gratitude practice, which could be very easily intertwined with the emotional check-ins and stretching routines we discussed earlier. Gratitude is known to bring us back to the present moment and help us find an anchor in times of distress or chaos.

There are fun and concrete ways to formalize a gratitude practice while teaching from a distance, too. In Chapter 7, we'll also discuss journaling, and journaling is a great way to have students log these moments of gratitude. I've also had my students create "gratitude chains," where they write gratitudes on long strips of paper, turning them into a paper chain. I've even had my students create gratitude trees where each gratitude takes the form of a leaf on a tree. As they add more gratitudes, they concretely see that they have a lot to be grateful for, instilling a sense of hope within them, even in times of crisis.

JUSTICE FOR TEACHERS

Centering socioemotional literacy matters not only for students. It matters for the adults in the room, too. And so I'll take a note from *Teaching Tolerance*, and encourage you to practice one strategy, in particular, that they recommend for giving yourself hope while getting through distance teaching in a global pandemic—as well as future storms we will have to weather as an educational community. This strategy is speaking truth to power.

Our kids deserve teachers who are cared for. Our kids deserve teachers whose lives are held in high regard. Our kids deserve teachers who feel empowered to stand up for themselves, their humanity, and the humanity of their students. Our kids deserve teachers who feel empowered to bring their whole selves into their classrooms—big, uncomfortable feelings and all. And they deserve teachers who are willing to advocate for all of this, especially when it's being threatened.

Speaking truth to power and standing up for myself gives me hope and has opened my eyes to a world of opportunity beyond the classroom. I hope that doing so—even in small, subtle ways—can give you hope for the future and help you take care of yourself in the process. And I hope that exercising this now will give you the courage to continue changing education for the better, even after the coronavirus pandemic is over.

TIPS FOR TEACHING FROM A DISTANCE, CHAPTER 2

- Center emotional well-being, not learning loss.

- Build predictable structures for daily schedules and learning block routines.

- Create visual schedules to help students keep track on their own.

- Schedule additional check-ins for students who are struggling, including "office hours" where students can come for extra help if they need it.

- Build emotional vocabulary by allowing students to talk about their feelings at the start of every learning block.

- Model how you communicate and process your feelings, normalizing them for students.

- Practice gratitude with your students through journaling.

- Speak truth to power and advocate for yourself if you feel you're being put in an unsafe situation. Your physical and emotional health and well-being matter, too.

CHAPTER THREE

BUILDING A RESILIENT CLASSROOM CULTURE

Our students will not become liberated learners or socially and emotionally conscious human beings if our classroom cultures do not reflect these values. A classroom environment where independence is expected and the skills that support independence are explicitly taught is a classroom environment where teachers can gradually remove scaffolds, allowing students to stand on their own. Just to be clear, this goes for in-person learning, too. The strategies in this book, while inspired by the harsh reality that so many of us are forced to teach through our computers, are really just best practices intended to reach students as human beings and empower them to step into their humanity.

Classroom cultures that value independence are built upon shared agreements and kept intact with the maintenance of these shared agreements. Classrooms that value independent learning cannot possibly operate without these classroom agreements. In classrooms that value independent learning, trust is a central mechanism to the classroom's operation. Students need to be trusted to work on their own, and to do so with respect for the collective. Without clearly stated agreements, it is unreasonable to expect that students can operate with independence, and this is even truer when teaching from a distance.

The Responsive Classroom (2015) approach, a widely used set of student-centered practices for socioemotional learning and classroom management, tells us that it's best to build these classroom agreements as a whole, and I couldn't agree more. Even though I had been teaching my class in person for seven whole months prior to the start of distance learning in the Spring of 2020, I still took the first week to build new classroom agreements with my students. I did this for obvious reasons. Our entire lives had been uprooted in less than a week. We had to take a moment to acknowledge the gravity of the situation and rebuild our classroom community in this very different, very digital space.

BUILDING AGREEMENTS ORGANICALLY

"I can't hear you, Mr. France!" one of my students said in one of our first virtual sessions. "There are so many little sounds." "Hmm, interesting," I replied. "How do you think we could fix that?"

It wasn't long until a student suggested that we use the muting function to turn off our own microphones when someone was talking.

"How does everyone feel about that?" I asked.

The students agreed that it was much easier to hear when others muted their microphones. Admittedly, I was wary to suggest this as a norm. I didn't want students to feel as though they were being silenced or muffled. While I generally requested that students not "blurt out" during in-person learning, it wasn't uncommon for a child's serendipitous, unfiltered thought to contribute something quite meaningful to a conversation. But in this case, all of the ancillary sounds were counterproductive to collaboration and whole-group learning.

As Responsive Classroom reminds us, building classroom norms should be a democratic and organic process, capitalizing on serendipitous moments like these. While we teachers know that certain structures and agreements will create a productive learning environment, we need to give our kids credit and remember that they, too, have ideas for how to make learning productive in a digital setting.

This moment in time was the perfect entry point to building agreements as a class, and as a result, over the next few days, the students and I collected a list of "little rules" that we'd need to follow in order to collaborate with one another in this digital space. They came up with quite a few rules, which I kept track of on a Google Slide that I projected through Google Meet. Here are some of them, in their words:

- Post to Seesaw activities, not to the journal.

- Always post to share work.

- Only use Google Hangouts with teacher permission.

- School-related things only.

- One emoji at a time.

- Stay on Meet the whole time.

- Stay muted so we can hear each other.

- Stay on topic.

- Only text with teachers' permission.

- If you're late, don't say hi in the chat.

- Use texting appropriately.

- Only use emojis when it's appropriate.

Naturally, we discussed how there were far too many rules to keep track of, and so, in true Responsive Classroom format, we came up with three "big, broad" rules that encompassed all of these agreements:

- Act like you're at school.

- Use the tools appropriately to help learning.

- Be a problem solver using the tools you have.

These broad rules allowed us to discuss new behaviors as distance learning progressed, encouraging students to ask themselves: Would they do that at school? Is that use of the tool helping them learn? Are you using the tools you have to problem-solve?

TAKING INTO ACCOUNT VARYING HOME LIVES

Building classroom agreements in this democratic and culturally responsive manner (Ladson-Billings,1994) was very important, albeit in different ways and for different reasons than if we were learning together in person. We have to remember that when we are engaging in distance learning, we are inevitably entering our students' homes, as Liz Kleinrock, educator, author, and creator of @TeachAndTransform, tells us (www.teachandtransform.org). For some students, we are welcomed guests, and for others we are not—and for a whole host of reasons. It doesn't make sense for all kids to keep their cameras on at all times, and if we are going to ask students to mute themselves, they must know there's a collective purpose in doing so—not that it's a means for controlling or silencing voices in the classrooms.

The fact is that entering students' homes makes *all* students feel vulnerable, even the ones who are welcoming it. We must not only be aware of this, we must be respectful of this and acknowledge the sanctity of entering a child's home without their permission. We must also resist the tendency to make assumptions about students' engagement based on what we can see and hear. Just because we can't see them or hear them doesn't mean they're not engaged.

This was especially hard for me. It didn't take long for me to realize just how much I had been relying on my students' body language to gauge their attentiveness, even though I knew very well that body language was not necessarily a reliable indicator of how much students were attending to instruction. But instead of creating a norm around camera usage, I used this new challenge as an opportunity to innovate. The uncertainty of student engagement encouraged me to keep my minilessons short, allowing me more time to check in with students in small-group calls on Google Hangouts or in one-on-one sessions. Even in these times where we checked in using small groups or one-on-one calls, I would always ask students' permission to turn their cameras on and respect a student's choice to keep it off.

In Chapter 6, we'll talk about redefining student success and humanizing assessment, and when we do, you will see that it's very possible to gauge student learning from a distance without invading students' privacy and forcing them to use the camera when they're uncomfortable.

RULES ARE MEANT TO BE BROKEN

Bear in mind that your classroom culture will change as the year goes on, and as a result, your classroom agreements will likely need to change, as well. Students will get into conflicts with one another, kids will get a bit too comfortable, and behaviors that disrupt collaboration will come out of the woodwork. As a result, I recommend using virtual morning meetings and/or closing circles to check in on classroom agreements and make changes as you see fit.

When we create ruthless sets of rigid rules, we operate in opposition to equity in our classrooms. Classrooms and their agreements are meant to evolve along with the class, and when we allow them to, our classrooms become purposeful and resilient places to teach and learn. The last thing you should do is remove students from your live learning sessions if they violate a norm. Consequences, as always, should be natural and restorative. If you're noticing that a given norm is repeatedly broken or overall just isn't working for your students, it might be time to use those morning meetings or closing circles to see if anyone has ideas for amendments to the agreements. If the agreement is necessary to the class's functioning, set a goal with the class and identify some strategies for success. At the end of the day, though, the norms should be supporting your class's ability to function, not limiting your students' abilities to connect with their peers and learn collaboratively. If your agreements aren't supporting this, it might be time to reevaluate them.

Nevertheless, if you keep equity at the center of your intentions for developing classroom norms, you will, without a doubt, be able to adjust your norms and continue teaching effectively from a distance.

NORMALIZING RISK, RUPTURE, AND REPAIR

I, too, found myself desperate for connection in the early Summer of 2020, and so I got creative. I contacted my good friend and fellow gay educator, Nate Lyon (@mr_lyon_4th), and asked him if he'd be interested in co-hosting a series on Instagram where we'd talk with LGBTQ+ educators from around the country, holding space to discuss the challenges and successes we've experienced as openly Queer educators.

The *Here and Queer Educator Series* was born in late June of 2020, and over the course of four weeks, Nate and I had the pleasure of speaking with twelve Queer educators from coast to coast. One educator, in particular, Finn Menzies (@teach_finn), a kindergarten teacher and man of trans experience, brought up the idea of *normalizing repair* in our classrooms. If our classrooms are going to be spaces where students are learning and growing, he conveyed, they will inevitably make mistakes.

But that's true for all of us. White educators across the country are reckoning with the apparent fact that we have a lot of learning to do. We must be talking about race and identity in our classrooms, and we must also be doing the hard work of unpacking our own identities so that we better understand our roles in systems of oppression. While we're learning—and we *always* will be learning—we will inevitably make mistakes, reveal our biases, and perhaps even cause harm in the process of building more equitable and courageous classrooms. When (not *if*) this happens, we need to be prepared to repair relationships and restore trust, for trust will be the fuel that keeps your classroom running, that is, if you are invested in student independence and liberation.

In my last book, *Reclaiming Personalized Learning*, I provided a four-step process for resolving conflicts in classrooms:

1. Assume positive intent.

2. Advocate for yourself.

3. Tell your story.

4. Get an adult if you need to.

I came to a realization this past year that assuming positive intent doesn't always work. In fact, assuming positive intent can be an act of violence against People of Color or LGBTQ+ people. When we tell children to assume positive intent in situations of clear bias or discrimination, we send a problematic message that instills a sense of self-doubt in them. Students of Color know racism when they see it; likewise, LGBTQ+ people can spot homophobia and transphobia easily. Instead of encouraging students to always assume positive intent, we should, instead, be encouraging them to get curious, to exercise a moment of mindfulness before reacting. This mindfulness allows students, as well as teachers, to assess their emotions and determine whether or not an escalated reaction is warranted. In the case of a physical or emotional threat related to racism, homophobia, sexism, or other forms of discrimination, a raised voice and anger may be warranted. In the case of a pencil borrowed without permission, that same anger may not be.

Regardless, we know these moments will happen in our classrooms—whether they are digital or in person, and as a result, in order for students to become independent learners who are liberated to think, speak, and act as they see fit, we have to be ready for these moments where conflicts arise and trust is ruptured. We cannot possibly build resilient classroom environments that incentivize risk-taking, mistake making, and vulnerability without modeling and normalizing repair.

I remember back to the beginning of the school year, as I was still learning students' names, I had repeatedly mixed up the names of two of my students in the first few weeks of school. Both of the students were Students of Color, and while I caught myself and fixed it, I noticed that my kids, including the two whose names I was juxtaposing, thought it was funny.

"It's okay, Mr. France," one of them said, "it's funny."

"I appreciate you being kind and letting me off the hook," I said to them. "But I don't think it's funny."

I could tell the tone in the classroom changed as a result of my direct words. Another Queer educator from our series, Derrick Carlson (@blackandbright in2nd), reminded us that when talking about normalizing repair we must model this for our students, especially if the rupture occurs in the context of the whole group.

"Names are important," I said to the entire class of students, "and it's my job to make sure I'm getting names right. I want you to know that your names really matter to me, and that I'm going to do a better job moving forward of thinking before I speak. I'm really sorry I've mixed up your names so many times now."

The children were, of course, compassionate and understanding. They forgave me, and I'm happy to say I was, in fact, more mindful moving forward. But in addition to teaching the students an important lesson that names matter and that mixing people up isn't okay, I also modeled for them how one apologizes and repairs relationships when they've ruptured them. Modeling self-accountability, remorse, and repair also serves as a means for implementing restorative justice practices within your classroom. In *These Kids Are Out of Control*, Rich Milner and his colleagues (2019) suggest a three-tiered pyramid for restorative discipline in classrooms, including affective language (language that authentically articulates emotions), circle processes (collective gatherings to address rupture or harm), and conferences (intended to resolve conflicts between individuals). Restorative discipline provides an excellent example of how we can intensify socioemotional work as a tool for student liberation—and not as a tool for weaponization or control. It centers all students' needs, as well as their humanity and right to a sense of belonging within the school community. But most of all, it serves as a concrete reminder that a healthy and resilient classroom culture is all about healthy and resilient relationships.

THE IMPORTANCE OF RELATIONSHIPS

We talk a lot about relationships now in education. This is a welcome change, but we must challenge ourselves to go beyond asking about student interests when building relationships. Trusting relationships are ones where all parties feel safe, where they feel that they can experience a broad range of emotions, where they feel they can step into their humanity and show up as their full selves. And this is why classroom culture matters, especially when it's being built digitally.

The fact is that a space isn't safe just because we say it is. Our actions and our words must exude safety, and when we do something to threaten that safety, we must address it to continue building trusting relationships with and between our students.

Our pedagogy must also be reflective of this resilient classroom culture where knowledge is constructed collaboratively and individual learners are encouraged to liberate themselves through self-awareness, self-advocacy, and the vulnerability that comes with heightened socioemotional awareness. Our pedagogy must be flexible and responsive; it must free itself of the industrialized mindset where students simply become consumers of content. It also must be healthily structured and sustainable so that we can manage an entire group of learners, from no matter where we teach.

TIPS FOR TEACHING FROM A DISTANCE, CHAPTER 3

- Build agreements organically and capitalize on problems that arise to have discussions about why classroom agreements are necessary.

- Create generalizable rules that can be applied to multiple contexts.

- Remember that rules are meant to be broken. Allow your agreements to evolve with your class.

- Normalize rupture and repair, modeling this for your students whenever possible.

- Remember that the key to building relationships is trust.

CHAPTER FOUR

MAKING PLANNING SUSTAINABLE

Teachers agree that planning for distance learning is challenging, perhaps even harder to prepare for than in-person learning. The transition was certainly an adjustment for me in the Spring of 2020, but take it from someone who had been teaching online long before the COVID-19 pandemic: Planning for digital learning doesn't have to be more complicated than teaching in person.

From 2014 to 2017, I worked for an education technology company and network of microschools in the Bay Area. My job had multiple purposes: I taught while helping develop digital tools for the classroom. Our charge was to personalize learning, and our means for achieving personalization were individualized playlists of activities, curated for students based on strengths, challenges, affinities, and interests. The idea was that by leveraging digital technology, we'd be able to personalize for diverse groups of students, using complex algorithms and data collection to make the process of personalizing sustainable. We never did manage to make the process sustainable. In fact, it was far more work than it was worth.

The problem with a vast majority of EdTech "solutions" is that they end up only making things more complicated. The clever marketing of education technology companies has convinced us that we need different applications for every subject, but I want to caution you against filling up your iPad, Chromebook, or other digital device with a whole bunch of useless applications. Planning for a humanized approach to distance learning shouldn't be all that much different than planning for a humanized approach to in-person learning. They key is to keep your planning learning oriented, as opposed to activity oriented, so you may remain flexible and responsive in your instruction, using your learning goals as a North Star to guide you through any uncertainty.

LEARNING-ORIENTED PLANNING

It was time for one of my (and generally speaking, my students') favorite units of the year. Unfortunately, we had just moved our entire curriculum online. I was worried that, by moving the unit online, it would be harder to conference with students, monitor their progress, and otherwise reach the same level of depth I had normally achieved teaching this unit. These fears were warranted, and if you are feeling the same way, your fears are warranted, too. My goal in writing this book is not to minimize or undermine the very real feelings that surface when having to reconfigure an entire curriculum for online learning; my goal, instead, is to let you know that you're not alone and that you can, in fact, get through this and still be effective. Ideally, your pedagogy will be forever changed for the better, allowing you to always teach from a distance, in the sense that you'll begin centering student independence more than you ever have before.

In our final writing unit of the year, my students and I adapted fairy tales, drawing from Lucy Calkins's Third-Grade Units of Study (2013). Truth be told, I'm not a big fan of following curriculum manuals, so I'm no stranger to using backward design to plan units of instruction. That said, I love Calkins's ideas. When creating units of instruction, she embraces a project-based approach, grounding reading and writing skills in authentic purposes.

When humanizing any sort of learning, it's always important to anchor it in some sort of greater purpose. Otherwise, kids don't understand why any given topic is important enough to learn. This is especially true for distance learning, as students run the risk of feeling even more disconnected from the collective consciousness of the class. We must make the purpose behind learning explicitly clear.

"Do you know why we study and adapt fairy tales?" I asked the students.

"Because they're fun?" one student replied.

"Sure, they're fun," I replied, "But that's not the only reason."

Even with more discussion and prompting, they came up short on reasons why we might choose to dedicate two whole months to adapting fairy tales, but truth be told, I didn't really expect them to know.

"Think back to the beginning of the year," I continued. "Do you remember what we discussed when we were studying stories and the lessons we can learn from them?"

"Yea!" one student exclaimed. "Stories are important because it's how people used to teach their children and pass down information and lessons."

"That's right," I replied. "Stories are really important. We don't read stories so you can answer questions on a test. We read stories because they teach us important lessons about being a good human being. And that's why we're studying fairy tales, too."

In the first series of lessons in our unit, I taught my students general facts about folktales and shared with them that fairy tales are merely a type of folktale with special characteristics. This was the main goal of our first series of lessons: I wanted students to understand the purpose of fairy tales and some of their key characteristics. Having taught the unit in prior years, I knew that it was quite easy for students to unknowingly "walk away" from the fairy tale genre while drafting their adaptations. They get overly excited, they want to be creative, and before anyone has realized otherwise, students write stories that hardly resemble the original fairy tale they were trying to adapt. I learned the first time I taught the unit that holding students accountable to identifying the characteristics of folktales and fairy tales was critical to writing a strong fairy tale adaptation.

"But there are some problems with fairy tales," I confided in them, "and that's also why we're writing fairy tale adaptations. Does anyone know why fairy tales can be problematic?"

Much to my surprise, one student volunteered an answer.

"A lot of fairy tales are about girls who need a prince to save them, and that's not good."

"Ah, yes," I replied, "lots of fairy tales have stereotypes in them, specifically gender stereotypes. And so, we have an opportunity when we adapt fairy tales to change them so they don't have those stereotypes in them anymore. We can put our own identities in them instead."

While, at the time, I hadn't yet been introduced to Gholdy Muhammad's (2020) four-layered framework for historically responsive literacy (HRL), a resource that we will revisit in Chapter 6 when we discuss redefining student success, it had occurred to me that this unit must be relevant to my students' identities. Not only was this a great way to continue unpacking identity far past the constraints of our initial unit on identity from September and October, it was an effective way to humanize the curriculum and make it personally relevant to them. When I first started teaching, I referred to this as "helping kids see themselves in the curriculum," but now, I see that it's simply another way to expand what we expect students to know and be able to do while engaging with literacy. Identity objectives should be a part of every learning experience, as Dr. Muhammad would tell us. Upon reflection, I now see that my unit had several identity objectives, including cultivating an awareness of stereotypes within fairy tales, as well as identifying ways for students to insert their own identities into fairy tales, rewriting them in their image.

You'll notice that when I talk about this unit, I discuss, first and foremost, what I want students to know and be able to do. While it's true that I identify those goals for myself, I also share them with my students, both in conversations and by using a written checklist of success criteria. I do this because it cultivates awareness around what we're learning and the purpose behind it, undoubtedly garnering investment, understanding, and even excitement from my students. They begin to understand that we're not learning about fairy tales or any other topic without reason or rationale. In the case of the fairy tales unit, they learned that fairy tales are an important part of history and that by adapting them, we are able to make positive, more inclusive, and socially just changes for the future.

I call this style of planning "learning oriented," but the idea of learning-oriented planning is not new. It is grounded in Wiggins and McTighe's *Understanding by Design* (2005), where teachers begin planning by identifying desired results, constructing assessment criteria, and planning instructional experiences accordingly, all with the goal of inching students toward the desired results.

Counterintuitively, planning with an activity-oriented mindset is actually quite a bit more challenging than planning with a learning-oriented mindset. In fact, I believe that it is this activity-oriented mindset that makes planning for distance learning unsustainable. Many educators operate by thinking, "I need to have something from them to do" or "I need something to keep them busy," as opposed to asking, "What set of learning experiences will keep my students engaged and working toward the desired results of the unit?" When planning with an activity-oriented mindset, educators suddenly feel pressured to "fill" the day with activities they will inevitably have to "grade," ultimately contributing to an ever-compounding workload that becomes unsustainable, and quite frankly, utterly useless for helping a child tell the story of their learning journey or documenting progress.

I've heard countless stories from parents that their remote learning experience from the spring was filled with worksheets and workbook pages, oftentimes leaving students feeling confused and frustrated because they hadn't enough exposure to the concepts required to complete the worksheets assigned. Again, this is not an indictment of the teachers who sent these worksheets home. In fact, some school districts and organizations required all work to be asynchronous, and in some cases, school administrations required busy work like this to be sent home. That said, we all know that completing worksheets and workbook pages isn't learning. Worksheets and workbook completion are indicative of an activity-oriented mindset, where teachers plan independently of learning objectives, and instead, plan with a dependence on an instructional resource, measuring their success by the number of pages completed or the percentage of the curriculum "covered."

In order for distance learning to be sustainable, we *must* move away from activity-oriented planning, and instead move toward a style of planning that first identifies learning goals before choosing or creating activities. The good news is that there are already tools out there for this. In the following sections, I will use Wiggins and McTighe's *Backward Design* approach to demonstrate how I thought about planning for distance teaching in a learning-oriented manner. This entails three steps: identifying desired results, collecting evidence, and writing a learning plan. I will use the aforementioned fairy tales unit, which was inspired and influenced by Lucy Calkins's Units of Study, to demonstrate how I use backward design to help me sustainably plan.

STAGE 1: IDENTIFYING DESIRED RESULTS

When taking a learning-oriented approach to planning for distance learning, we begin by identifying the desired results (see Figure 4.1 on the next page). You'll notice I've used the Common Core Literacy Standards to identify established goals, as well as the Teaching Tolerance Framework, a framework of Social Justice standards categorized into identity, diversity, justice, and action standards.

Established Goals

CCSS.ELA-LITERACY.RL.3.2

Recount stories, including fables, folktales, and myths from diverse cultures; determine the central message, lesson, or moral and explain how it is conveyed through key details in the text.

CCSS.ELA-LITERACY.W.3.3

Write narratives to develop real or imagined experiences or events using effective technique, descriptive details, and clear event sequences.

CCSS.ELA-LITERACY.W.3.3.A

Establish a situation and introduce a narrator and/or characters; organize an event sequence that unfolds naturally.

CCSS.ELA-LITERACY.W.3.3.B

Use dialogue and descriptions of actions, thoughts, and feelings to develop experiences and events or show the response of characters to situations.

CCSS.ELA-LITERACY.W.3.3.C

Use temporal words and phrases to signal event order.

CCSS.ELA-LITERACY.W.3.3.D

Provide a sense of closure.

CCSS.ELA-LITERACY.L.3.2

Demonstrate command of the conventions of standard English capitalization, punctuation, and spelling when writing.

Teaching Tolerance (ID.3-5.1)

I know and like who I am and can talk about my family and myself and describe our various group identities.

Teaching Tolerance (JU.3-5.11)

I try and get to know people as individuals because I know it is unfair to think all people in a shared identity are the same. (stereotypes)

Transfer

Students will be able to identify adaptations of common fairy tales and write their own after identifying the essential elements of stories.

Meaning

Understandings	Essential Question
Fairy tales are outdated and promote stereotypes. By writing ourselves into them, we can re-create them in our image and be more inclusive.	Why do fairy tale adaptations matter?

Acquisition

Knowledge (Declarative)	Skill (Procedural)
Key Vocabulary: • adaptation • fairy tale • folktale • dialogue • sensory details • revise • edit Students will be able to • identify the characteristics of folktales and fairy tales. • identify the essential elements of a given fairy tale.	Students will be able to • use the structure of a fairy tale to create an adaptation. • write strong openings using dialogue and sensory details. • develop the story using dialogue, sensory details, and revision strategies. • use transition words and phrases to move between scenes. • punctuate dialogue correctly using quotation marks and commas. • paragraph text and indent properly. • edit for spelling, capitalization, and punctuation.

Source: Adapted from Wiggins & McTighe, 2005; Calkins et al. 2013.

STAGE 2: COLLECTING EVIDENCE

In Chapter 7, we'll talk at length about redefining success by humanizing assessment while teaching from a distance. Identifying methods for collecting evidence, as well as a schedule for doing so is critical and will make planning for distance learning sustainable. Identifying methods for collecting evidence prior to planning instructional experiences is also an indicator that you are taking a learning-oriented approach to distance teaching, as opposed to an activity-oriented one. By first identifying a cadence for collecting evidence, as well as the media or activities through which you will be doing so, you may construct learning experiences in a manner that lets your class gradually build to those assessment points, using the learning goals and formative assessments to guide everyday decision-making and next steps. While specific milestones for evidence collection are not stated in Stage 2 (Figure 4.2), they appear in Stage 3 (Figure 4.3).

Figure 4.2: Stage 2 (Collecting Evidence)

Evaluative Criteria	Performance Tasks
• Narrative Writing Checklist, incorporating success criteria • Single-Point Rubric (Dietz, 2000; Fluckiger, 2010; Gonzalez, 2015), related to checklist items	• Fairy Tale Adaptation of Cinderella (Collected in Week 4, assessed using checklist) • Fairy Tale Adaptation (Students choose fairy tale; collected in Week 6/7, assessed using checklist)
	Other Evidence
	• Weekly writing samples, submitted in Seesaw each Friday to gauge pace and progress • Anecdotal notes from writing conferences

Source: Adapted from Wiggins & McTighe, 2005; Calkins et al., 2013.

STAGE 3: BUILDING THE LEARNING PLAN

By first identifying desired results and the means for collecting evidence, teachers are liberated from day-to-day planning, and can instead plan in arcs of instruction. These arcs are not dominated by activities that must be graded or tallied every day; instead, they are governed by each child's respective level of mastery, in relation to the desired results identified for the unit of instruction. Because daily lessons are not influenced by compliance metrics or governed by arbitrary work completion, teachers are free to be flexible and responsive with their teaching, not only to create new minilessons in response to student misconceptions, but also to modify individual students' workloads if they require a modified learning path.

In the example below, you'll notice that I plan in terms of weeks (or arcs) with a menu of suggested learning activities. The menu of learning activities helps me brainstorm ideas for lessons I anticipate I'll need to teach, as opposed to a linear path of lessons that I feel obligated to teach. Within each week or arc, I have a clear learning goal, knowing full well that each activity I do will support my goal for the week. I also go into each week knowing that I may not teach all of the lessons. I empower myself to leave out lessons if time does not permit, or if I come to believe my students don't need them.

In some cases, it may even make sense to have multiple learning goals for one week, depending on the depth and breadth of each learning goal. It's also important to note that I list my lessons in the order I anticipate that I'll teach them. That said, these learning plans can easily be adjusted. I know

Figure 4.3: Stage 3 (Learning Plan)

	Summary of Key Learning Events
Dates	**Learning Plan**

Week/ Arc 1	Students will be able to identify key characteristics of fairy tales, including magical elements, the presence of good and evil, threes, and other elements they discover.
	
	Learning Activities for Minilessons:
	
	• Narrative Preassessment (Evidence)
	• Unpack/Review Narrative Writing Checklist.
	• Create Folktales Tree Map (Hyerle, 1995) to discuss types of folktales and fairy tales.
	• Create Circle Map (Hyerle, 1995) for Characteristics of Fairy Tales (Multiple Lessons).
	  ○ Three Billy Goats Gruff (Read Aloud and Add to Circle Map)
	  ○ Cinderella (Read Aloud and Add to Circle Map)

Week/ Arc 2	Students will identify ways to adapt fairy tales, including adapting the setting, the problem, the main character, or the character's motivation. Learning Activities for Minilessons: • Read Cinderelle (Calkins, Frazin, & Roberts, 2013) or another Cinderella adaptation and discuss how fairy tales can be adapted by changing the setting or the main problem.

Dates	Learning Plan
	• Read aloud *Prince Cinders* (Cole, 1987) and discuss how the fairy tale has been adapted by changing the main character in terms of gender or other group identity.
	• Model structures for changing elements of fairy tales (single lesson; model options)
	○ Flow Map (Hyerle, 1995) to show how sequence of events changes
	○ Multi-Flow Map (Hyerle, 1995) to show cause and effect relationship between changes
	• Brainstorm ways to start Opening Scenes using Try Ten (Buckner, 2005).
	• Unpack single-point rubric (Dietz, 2000; Fluckiger, 2010; Gonzalez, 2015) for openings (evidence) and reflect on progress; collect writing sample.
Week/ Arc 3	Students will structure their first fairy tale adaptation by identifying the key elements of their fairy tale and mapping out the scenes. If time permits, students will begin drafting scenes. Learning Activities for Minilessons: • Analyze success criteria on the writing checklist and help students set writing goals. Model how to use the Flow Map for sketching out story scenes. • Model how to draft an opening scene using sensory details and dialogue (shared writing). • Model how to revise writing in order to add sensory details and dialogue (Review Lifting a Line [Buckner, 2005]). • Brainstorm lists of transition words and demonstrate how to revise by adding transition words and phrases. • Generate ideas for endings with shared writing. • Model how to revise confusing sentences (Review Try Ten [Buckner, 2005]). • Unpack single-point rubric (Dietz, 2000; Fluckiger, 2010; Gonzalez, 2015) for story development (evidence) and reflect on progress; collect writing sample.
Week/ Arc 4	Students will edit and revise their writing for proper capitalization, ending punctuation, punctuating dialogue, indenting paragraphs, and spelling. Learning Activities for Minilessons: • Brainstorm a list of places to indent using a section of Mr. France's story; model how to indent. • Practice punctuating Mr. France's dialogue and inserting paragraphs.

(Continued)

Dates	Learning Plan
	• Have students share words they are curious about and would like to explore as a class; complete word matrices for these selected words.
	• Complete the checklist after finishing the fairy tale adaptation; reflect on progress and set new goals.
	• Share writing with peers, practicing giving and receiving feedback on their writing.
Week/ Arc 5	Students will begin adapting a new fairy tale with increased independence, using feedback from their first fairy tale to set goals. Learning Activities for Minilessons: • Provide students time to explore other fairy tales and identify essential elements using Flow Maps. • Reflect on first fairy tale, identifying celebrations, challenges, and action steps (complete reflection template). • Review Multi-Flow and Flow Maps (Hyerle, 1995) for making small changes to characters, setting or plot of fairy tales. • Review single-point rubrics for strong opening and story development; engage class in shared writing experience to start a new fairy tale adaptation. • Collect work samples and assess using single-point rubrics (Dietz, 2000; Fluckiger, 2010; Gonzalez, 2015); submit with self-reflection and work samples on Seesaw.
Week/ Arc 6/7	Students will revise, edit, and publish their writing, using the checklist and Single-Point Rubrics to analyze their work. Learning Activities for Minilessons: • Review habits for sharing writing with peers; re-model how to give and receive feedback. • Identify lines to revise and how to choose between revising strategies (Lift a Line and Try Ten [Buckner, 2005]). • Review single-point rubrics (Dietz, 2000; Fluckiger, 2010; Gonzalez, 2015) in conferences to assist students in making changes to their work. • Celebrate learning with a publishing party (using checklist and peer feedback for final reflection).

Source: Adapted from Wiggins & McTighe, 2005; Calkins et al., 2013.

that some teachers prefer to have a more defined schedule with dates. Others are more comfortable with a more general framework like the one depicted in Figure 4.3. Teachers should feel empowered to adjust these outlines in a way that makes sense to them, adding layers of specificity as they see fit.

Notice how, in my learning plan above, each of the activities supports a clearly defined objective for the week, but that the list of activities does not pigeonhole my teaching into a rigid or linear set of learning experiences. Instead, the flexible structure of the plans allows me to pivot as needed and change my plans to help me reach my end-of-week goal. If, by chance, I notice I need more time on a given weekly goal, I can very easily turn one week into a week and a half or two, changing the dates that I collect the work samples, ultimately providing me with the flexibility I desire and the responsiveness my students need in order to learn from a distance and with independence. This is also why I refer to them as "weeks" and "arcs" interchangeably: sometimes an arc will take more than a week, and it's important to me to make sure my students have learned what I want them to before moving on to the next arc.

FLEXIBILITY AND RESPONSIVENESS

Invariably, I have a few students who move more quickly than the remainder of the class, and conversely, I have a handful of students who move at a pace more gradual than the majority. During in-person learning, it's rather easy to ask students who finish quickly to start writing a new story, read independently, or play a math game, but with distance learning, it's a bit more challenging, given the constraints around materials and the fact that I can't physically see them at all times.

One student, in particular, chose an unintended path while writing their fairy tale in the Spring. Jo, who identified as non-binary and used the pronoun "they," had a very strong oral vocabulary which translated smoothly into their writing. They found it easy to be creative when writing stories, and as a result, they used their spare time in the first week's lessons to get started on drafting, a choice I had offered to all students. By the time we reached the end of Arc 2 of our learning plan, Jo already had a great deal of their story done! It took me by surprise, but I was impressed by their level of independence and forethought.

When I reviewed Jo's work, I noticed that they had written their story with a great amount of detail. I was thrilled to see they were applying our lessons on revising from previous units, using revising strategies such as Try Ten or Lift a Line (Buckner, 2005) to describe the setting in-depth. But there was a small issue. They were going so in-depth that it was slowing them down, and by the end of the following week, they didn't seem on track with our class plan to complete a first draft by the end of the month. What's more, they had inadvertently neglected to complete one of the assignments, the Flow Map, outlined in the learning plan from the week prior and intended to scaffold the process of structuring the story, ensuring it had all of the essential elements of the fairy tale they were adapting. Jo had historically struggled to finish their work by the agreed-upon deadlines during in-person learning, and I knew that distance learning would only exacerbate these challenges.

"Can you tell me a little bit about the structure of your story?" I asked Jo one day in a writing conference. "I noticed you never finished the Flow Map from last week."

They very succinctly rattled off all of the key details of their Cinderella adaptation, complete with all plot points and essential components of a Cinderella adaptation. While there was a part of me that wanted Jo to go back and complete the Flow Map that the rest of the students had, I reminded myself to teach in a learning-oriented manner, not with an activity-based mindset. When I considered the function of the Flow Map, it was never intended to be a compliance tool; it was intended to be scaffold for helping my students structure their stories. And it was clear in this conference that Jo didn't need that scaffold, rendering the activity useless and perhaps even counterproductive to their process. What was most important was that Jo finish their story in a timely manner so they could share their story with their classmates.

"You know what?" I said to them after hearing their succinct summary of their story, demonstrating to me that they understood story structure and how to apply it to a fairy tale. "I can see that you have a good plan for your story, and so that might mean that you don't need to do the Flow Map. How do you feel about skipping that step and continuing with drafting? You seem like you're on a roll."

I could immediately sense a change in their demeanor, as if a weight had been lifted off of their shoulders. Being behind and missing deadlines caused them stress, that was for sure, and being relieved of yet another activity, which would have, without a doubt, been a tool for compliance, not only kept their momentum up, it helped them see that I was on their side, too. It reminded them, albeit subtly, that this writing project was about the learning—not the activities themselves.

I sent them on their virtual way, and despite the modification to their workload, Jo hadn't quite finished their story for the peer feedback session we scheduled at the end of the following week. But this, too, served as a talking point in our writing conference, harkening back to Chapter 1 where we discussed independent learning habits. I was able to talk with Jo about what they might do differently for the second fairy tale adaptation. They agreed that if they were behind the "group plan," a term Michelle Garcia Winner coined in her book *Think Social! A Social-Thinking Curriculum for School Age Students* (2008), that they would spend some time in the evenings working on their own to finish on time.

A few weeks later, Jo had their final story ready for our publishing party, holding themself accountable to finishing. Bear in mind this was not out of compliance; it was because Jo wanted to connect with their classmates and share a completed story. Completing the story, ultimately, was about a human experience—a publishing party celebration in which Jo wanted to partake. It was about the humanity of it.

DAY-TO-DAY PLANNING

You may very well be wondering about day-to-day lesson plans. In truth, many teachers choose not to write down detailed daily lesson plans. Most experienced teachers I know may write down a brief sentence or short blurb in their lesson plans but always keep in mind their learning objectives. That's not to say that you shouldn't flesh out daily lesson plans in great detail if you find such scaffolding useful. In the example I provide in Figure 4.4, you'll notice that I go into great detail about the steps I will take in the lesson. This is intended to provide an example for teachers who are looking for more support with planning. All teachers should feel empowered to plan in a manner that provides them clarity and helps them operate with intention.

In Chapter 7, we'll discuss complex instruction, a style of pedagogy that can guide lesson planning during distance learning, hopefully making preparation for virtual lessons sustainable and allowing you to spend the majority of your energy focused on connecting with kids, as opposed managing applications or grading student work. When planning individual lessons within any subject area, I consider the following five questions:

- What do I hope students will leave knowing or able to do?

- How will I know if students understand, know, or are able to do this?

- What instructional resource will I use to provoke curiosity and discussion?

- How will I facilitate the discussion or minilesson?

- How will I reflect on the lesson with my students?

I use this five-question planning structure because it very closely reflects backward design, only on a more granular level. This flexible structure also guides me if ever I feel lost mid-lesson. The first question, *What do I hope students will leave knowing or be able to do?* is analogous to the "Desired Results" section of the unit-planning template. The second question, *How will I know if students understand, know, or are able to do this?* is reminiscent of Stage 2 of backward design, collecting evidence. Questions 3 and 4 represent the learning plan portion of backward design, where teachers choose instructional resources and anticipate student responses. Questions 3 and 4 also allow learning to take a student-driven and inquiry-based approach, liberating students and teachers alike from a didactic pedagogy that centers rote memorization. Question 5 centers student self-reflection, a critical component to building self-awareness and self-advocacy in the learning process. It also becomes assessment *as* learning (Gottlieb, 2016), meaning it's both a learning activity and an indicator of progress.

In Figure 4.4, I've adapted these five questions into a template, and I'll use a lesson from Arc 2, where students grapple with changing elements of the original Cinderella fairy tale to create a new story. As I previously mentioned, this can be tricky for kids, as many of them tend to "walk away" from the fairy tale. Helping them see the connection between events is critical to success in this unit.

Figure 4.4: Five-Question Lesson Planning Template (Cinderella Adaptations)

Question 1: What do I hope students will leave knowing or be able to do?

Students will understand that, by changing an element of Cinderella for their adaptation, other elements will need to change.

Question 2: How will I know if students understand, know, or are able to do this?

Students will submit a Flow Map or Multi-Flow Map on Seesaw as a formative assessment.

Question 3: What instructional resource will I use to provoke curiosity and discussion?

We use our knowledge of Prince Cinders (Cole, 1987), the previous day's read aloud, to identify ways in which the author changed the story.

Question 4: How will I facilitate the discussion or minilesson?

Together, through sharing and dialogue, we will brainstorm some ways we can change the story. I will document these ideas on two different Thinking Maps: the Multi-Flow Map and the Flow Map (Hyerle, 1995).

i. Activate background knowledge by asking students what they remember from Prince Cinders. How did the author change the story? Share with students that today they will be learning how making small changes to a story will change other parts of the story.

2. Using the Multi-Flow Map, model a new story idea. Ask students ways to adapt the fairy tale by changing essential elements, and then create an "If . . ." statement. For instance, "If I change the motivation to going to a baseball game, instead of a ball . . ."

3. Then, ask them how the rest of the story would change, filling these ideas in on the Multi-Flow Map. For example, "Then the main character will want to be chosen for the baseball team, instead of being chosen as the Prince's wife." or "Then the main character's siblings will be invited to a baseball game, instead of a ball."

Figure 4.4a: Multi-Flow Map

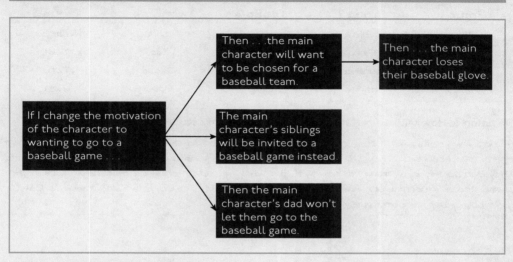

Source: Adapted from Hyerle, 1995.

Share what this might look like with a Flow Map, too, clarifying the difference between the two: one shows sequence, while the other is meant for cause-and-effect relationships. Casually ask students which of the tools makes more sense to them today, and allow them to pick between the two.

Figure 4.4b: Flow Map

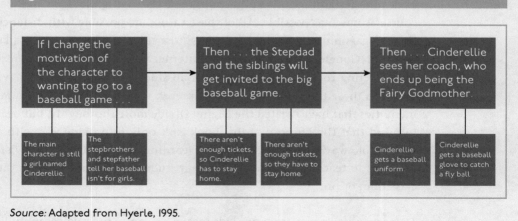

Source: Adapted from Hyerle, 1995.

(Continued)

After, allow students to begin work on their own. Clearly communicate that the expectation is for students to complete one of the two maps. If they finish early, they may begin drafting or make a second (or third) map to play with ideas. The remainder of discussions will be facilitated in Google Hangouts in small groups, allowing for peer-to-peer feedback and individualized feedback. Students will be encouraged to go into their groups ahead of time and talk about their stories in their hangouts.

Student groupings (all names are pseudonyms)

Group 1	Group 2	Group 3	Group 4	Group 5
Alex	Ellie	Imani	Monroe	Rodrigo
Bella	Fiona	Jo	Nia	Suri
Cole	Gunther	Kira	Oscar	Tiana
Darius	Henry	Linus	Pablo	Zari

Question 5: How will we reflect on this lesson with my students?

Students will return to the asynchronous learning session to share their work, as well as give or receive feedback. They will also share challenges they have and what their next steps are. They can do this by sharing verbally with the whole group or entering their next steps in the chat. Once all student work has been collected on Seesaw, students will be allowed to leave the whole-group synchronous video conference session.

ADAPTING LESSONS TO DISTANCE LEARNING

The reason that these lessons are so easily adapted to distance learning is because they are grounded in best practice. They leverage core high-impact pedagogies like framing learning goals in student-friendly language, backward-designing units and lessons, and leveraging dialogue and discourse as much as possible. All of these things are possible with distance learning, assuming that you have access to a video conferencing tool like Zoom or Google Meet and a stable internet connection. I'd be remiss in neglecting to acknowledge that not all students in our country have access to these tools currently. In Chapter 9, we'll discuss the structural inequities that have created the Digital Divide more thoroughly, but bear in mind that the purpose of this book isn't only to provide you with a sustainable way to approach distance learning; it's also to discuss what it means to teach at a distance from our students, whether we're in the classroom or not.

To teach at a distance from our kids means we center their voices in mini-lessons through dialogue, and it means we plan in a manner that's flexible and responsive to the independent choices they might make while working. But it also means that we invest our trust in them, allowing them to venture off on their own and work without our eyes constantly affixed to them. This is even more challenging to do during distance learning, as we can't simply redirect them when we see them off-task out of the corners of our eyes. All the more reason why, when teaching and learning at a distance, it is so important to build a strong classroom culture, to check in with students frequently in small-group and through individual conferences, and to ensure that you are collecting digital work samples frequently enough to stay up to date on their progress. It's also why it's important to make sure they know what to do if they encounter an obstacle or are unsure of what to do next.

"Remember everyone," I like to say, "a writer's work is never done."

My students quickly learn that this means I expect them to be writing for the entirety of our writing workshop session. If they finish early, they're expected to draft a new piece, edit, or revise. The same applies for other subjects. If they finish a reading assignment early, they are expected to work through their book bins or other independent reading material. If they finish a math task early, they are expected to approach the problem from a different angle, using a different method or strategy. These options are possible both in distance learning and during in-person learning. The worst-case scenario? Students take a much earned—and likely much needed—break while they're waiting for others to finish. It's a common misconception that students must be engaged at all minutes of the day, but the reality is that those expectations are likely grounded in our desire to control and micromanage our students' every move. Providing some simple after-work choices and allowing for rest are perfectly reasonable if students happen to finish early. Just make sure to communicate these expectations clearly.

Ultimately, the only core difference between distance learning and in-person learning should be the tools you use to facilitate whole-group experiences, meet in small groups, conference with students individually, and manage student work. Too many teachers believe that virtual pedagogy and in-person pedagogy are two entirely different types of learning, requiring an entirely different skillset, but I find this to be a misconception. In-person pedagogy and virtual pedagogy are both effective if we use the workshop model and complex instruction to make learning multi-dimensional, deindustrialize curriculum, and hold sacred the notion of teaching for liberation, all of which we'll discuss after we discuss the first and perhaps most important unit you should plan for the year—your identity study.

TIPS FOR TEACHING FROM A DISTANCE, CHAPTER 4

- Plan with a learning-oriented mindset, not an activity-oriented one.

- Resist the urge to download a bunch of apps to plan for distance learning.

- Share with students the purpose behind units and lessons. Connect this purpose to students' humanity.

- Use backward design to plan units.

- When creating learning plans, allow yourself a flexible structure that grants you ample opportunities to pivot.

- Adjust students workloads when they're standing in the way of learning.

- Use the Five-Question Planning Template for day-to-day planning, and keep it in mind when you're teaching on the fly.

- Embrace a project-based approach with an essential question, open-ended tasks, and lots of dialogue, discourse, and collaboration.

CHAPTER FIVE

UNPACKING IDENTITY

When I first started teaching, I was afraid to be outed, worried that my identity as a homosexual man would work against me and erode trust between my families and me. My fears were realized in the 2013–2014 school year when my colleague, Markus, and I experienced significant repercussions for proposing a marriage equality lesson to families, shortly after it had been legalized in Illinois. While my superintendent and principal tried to reassure me that it was "nothing personal," and that families just weren't ready to talk about the LGBTQ+ community in their predominantly white, affluent suburb, I couldn't help but take it personally.

Erasure is really common in a white supremacist, heteronormative, and patriarchal culture. It allows us to ignore what we don't want to see—that which makes us uncomfortable. That is what my administrators were really saying to me in that first job.

Your full identity makes us uncomfortable, so we're going to erase parts of it to make us feel better.

It's heartbreaking to experience this, and it causes people like me to pre-emptively erase themselves in schools. That way, at least, someone else isn't choosing erasure on our behalf. The potential for erasure is even greater now that many students are forced to learn from their homes. It's now even easier for our students to recede into the background, hidden behind a black screen and a muted microphone. As teachers, we must be aware of this, and we must make every effort possible to help our students feel like they want to turn their cameras on, unmute their microphones, and share themselves with their classroom community.

In some ways, we are fortunate to be living in a time of great change. Those who've been erased are no longer willing to be. As a gay man, I understand LGBTQ+ erasure, and I know the emotional labor required to make myself seen each year. As a white man, I do not know the feeling of racial and ethnic erasure, but I know that it exists. I know that our curricula are whitewashed, intended to tell stories and teach skills that benefit white people and marginalize Students of Color. I know that movies and TV shows disproportionately represent whiteness and white experiences, despite the fact that our country (and classrooms) grow less and less white by the day. And I know that these realities we live with today were consciously engineered by the forefathers of the United States who wrote the United States Constitution for white, male landowners. It took hundreds of years for subsequent groups to be "amended in." While most U.S. history books tell a different story, America was built on white supremacist values—values that have undergirded our most sacred institutions including the way we do school. At this particular point in our history when many white Americans are waking up to the realities of racial injustice, it shouldn't take much convincing that discussions of identity have an important place in our classrooms. Having such conversations with our students as well as our peers is the first step toward dismantling our prevailing systems of oppression and restoring equity to our schools and society at large.

Despite the comforting reality that, upon returning to Chicago, I was working for a school that accepted me as an openly gay man, I still didn't feel comfortable coming out my first year. And to this day, as I work with new families and new students, I experience feelings of trepidation when I think about revealing my true identity as a gay man.

So why do I do it? Why do I subject myself to the anxiety and distress this brings? I do it because I believe it's important to share our full identities with our students, that is, if the environment is safe enough to do so. No matter what my critics might say, I know that young children are able to comprehend same-sex relationships. Experience has taught me it is, in fact, developmentally appropriate to teach students about adult relationships, and that we don't have to wait until they're older to do so.

This goes for discussions on race, ethnicity, socioeconomic status, or any other indicator of identity. Children are old enough to have conversations about identity, and they are sophisticated enough to begin understanding how marginalized identities experience less power and privilege than dominant identities. In a world where Black lives matter, where love is love, and where trans rights are human rights, it is our moral imperative to teach about identity—even when teaching from a distance.

In many ways, to study identity means to learn from a distance. When someone identifies differently than us, it may very well feel like they are worlds apart, living a life that is unrecognizable to us. However, by intentionally studying identity, we grant ourselves and our students the opportunity to close that distance or perhaps simply build bridges between these seemingly different worlds, setting our students up to learn on their own and equipped with the necessary skills to understand diverse perspectives, stories, and people.

IDENTITY STUDIES

The first unit you plan each year should include an identity study. More than ever, it's critical that we study identity so students can learn through a lens that is culturally relevant—a term coined by Gloria Ladson-Billings (1994). I like to start each school year by reading *All Are Welcome* by Alexandra Penfold and Suzanne Kaufman (2018). It's a book that's easily accessible to all students. While Penfold's words share a beautiful message of inclusivity, Kaufman's pictures share even more. In the book, all sorts of identities are on display as a provocation for discussion about the different types of people we encounter in the world around us. Figure 5.1 shows what this looks like using the Five-Question Planning Template from Chapter 4.

Figure 5.1: Five-Question Lesson Planning Template

Question 1: What do I hope students will leave knowing or be able to do?

Students will be able to name aspects of identity, including but not limited to the following words: "race," "ethnicity," "socioeconomic status," "gender," "sexuality," "religion," or "language."

Question 2: How will I know if students understand, know, or are able to do this?

Before and after the read aloud, I will collect work samples to gauge prerequisite knowledge on identity. Before the read aloud, students will write words or phrases on sticky notes, answering the question What makes you who you are? After the lesson, students will write a thinking journal entry that shares how their thinking changed over the course of the lesson. They will use the thinking routine, "I used to think . . . Now I think . . ." (Ritchhart, Church, & Morrison, 2011) as a scaffold for reflection. They will be allowed to use a different structure if they do not need the scaffold.

Question 3: What instructional resource will I use to provoke curiosity and discussion?

All Are Welcome by Alexandra Penfold and Suzanne Kaufman (2018)

Question 4: How will I facilitate the discussion or minilesson?

Students will begin by putting their sticky notes on our class Circle Map (Hyerle, 2015) on the front easel. As we read the story, students will assist in adding to our Circle Map when they find more words that articulate someone's identity (i.e., "hijab," "transgender," "Black").

(Continued)

Circle Map

I will also use "turn and talk" to have students reflect with peers while reading the story to facilitate interpersonal discussions. If this lesson takes place in distance learning, I will allow students to use the chat function to submit ideas. I will also have the students use break-out groups of two or three to discuss.

I imagine that students will come with varying background knowledge and at times I will have to provide them with the language necessary to discuss identity. I anticipate sharing words like "gender," "sexuality," "race/ethnicity," or other group identifiers. I also anticipate potentially having to speak with students about "oops" moments. If I do, I will share with them that sometimes when talking about identity we make mistakes and hurt someone else's feelings. When they do this, it's important to acknowledge the person's feelings, apologize, share what they've learned, and identify what they'll do differently next time.

Question 5: How will we reflect on this lesson with my students?

Students will use "I used to think . . . Now I think . . ." to reflect on this discussion. I will begin by modeling this thinking routine in my thinking journal, providing them some inspiration for what to write. Depending on the discussion, I may write the following:

- I used to think that identity was about interests, but now I know that identity is includes things like gender and where you live.

- I used to think it was scary to talk about race, now I know that I need to talk about it, even if it makes me uncomfortable.

For students who require additional support, I will encourage them to write down one of my reflections and either change or add to the reflection, in an effort to get them used to the thinking routine. This may be necessary if they've never seen the routine or are experiencing uncertainty as we start the new year.

It's important to remember that no lesson takes place in isolation, and this is especially true for identity studies. Lessons should be connected to one another, gradually building toward a deeper and more nuanced understanding of the topics to be studied. Figure 5.2 provides a sample cross-disciplinary unit for studying identity to start the school year to help you see how this might unfold over the first month of school. You'll notice that in the unit, I categorize activities into two categories: literacy and social studies. I did this because, in the school I worked when developing these activities, I had separate blocks for literacy and social studies. In a perfect world, I wouldn't need to separate these activities. Everything would be blended together. That said, many of us are forced to teach in subjects, reserving parts of the day for literacy and others for social studies. I encourage you to structure your learning plan in a way that works for your schedule.

Figure 5.2: Sample Unit on Identity

Stage I (Desired Results)

Established Goals	Transfer	
CCSS.ELA-LITERACY.W.3.3 Write narratives to develop real or imagined experiences or events using effective technique, descriptive details, and clear event sequences.	Students will understand that identity impacts every facet of their lives and the lives of their peers.	
	Meaning	
	Understandings	**Essential Question**
CCSS.ELA-LITERACY.W.3.3.A Establish a situation and introduce a narrator and/or characters; organize an event sequence that unfolds naturally.	There are lots of things that make me who I am. Some of these things will change, and some of them will stay the same—but they are all important to who I am.	What makes you who you are?
CCSS.ELA-LITERACY.W.3.3.B Use dialogue and descriptions of actions, thoughts, and feelings to develop experiences and events or show the response of characters to situations.	**Acquisition**	
	Knowledge (Declarative)	**Skill (Procedural)**
CCSS.ELA-LITERACY.W.3.3.C Use temporal words and phrases to signal event order. CCSS.ELA-LITERACY.W.3.3.D Provide a sense of closure.	Key Vocabulary • Identity • Group identity • Role • Race/ethnicity • Religion	Students will be able to • write personal narrative stories that have a beginning, middle, and end and share about what makes them who they are.

(Continued)

Established Goals	Transfer	
	Acquisition	
CCSS.ELA-LITERACY.L.3.2	**Knowledge (Declarative)**	**Skill (Procedural)**
Demonstrate command of the conventions of standard English capitalization, punctuation, and spelling when writing.	• LGBTQ+ • Socioeconomic status • Sexual orientation • Gender • Language • Spiritual affiliation	• edit and revise stories to clarify their message. • compare and contrast identities to identify similarities and differences.
Teaching Tolerance (ID.3-5.1)		
I know and like who I am and can talk about my family and myself and describe our various group identities.		
Teaching Tolerance (ID.3-5.2)	Students will be able to	• share positive things about others' identities.
I know about my family history and culture and about current and past contributions of people in my main identity groups.	• identify parts of their own identities. • explain the difference between group identities, roles, small moments, family history, and traits.	• share parts of their family histories that they are comfortable bringing into the class.
Teaching Tolerance (ID.3-5.3)		
I know that all my group identities are part of who I am, but none of them fully describes me and this is true for other people too.		• ask questions about peers to get to know them better
Teaching Tolerance (ID.3-5.4)		
I can feel good about my identity without making someone else feel badly about who they are.		• reflect on "oops" moments and repair relationships when they make a mistake talking about identity.
Teaching Tolerance (ID.3-5.5)		
I know my family and I do things the same as and different from other people and groups, and I know how to use what I learn from home, school, and other places that matter to me.		
Teaching Tolerance (DI.3-5.7)		
I have accurate, respectful words to describe how I am similar to and different from people who share my identities and those who have other identities.		
Teaching Tolerance (DI.3-5.8)		
I want to know more about other people's lives and experiences, and I know how to ask questions respectfully and listen carefully and non-judgmentally		

Stage 2 (Collecting Evidence)

Evaluative Criteria	Performance Tasks
• Narrative Writing Checklist, incorporating success criteria • Single Point Rubric, related to writing checklist items • Checklist for "I Am . . ." Poems	• Personal Narrative Stories • "I Am . . ." Poems • Identity Murals
	Other Evidence
	• Weekly writing samples, submitted in Seesaw each Friday to gauge pace and progress • Anecdotal notes from writing conferences • Thinking Journal Responses • Sticky Notes and Anchor Charts from class discussions

Stage 3 (Learning Plan)

Summary of Key Learning Events

Dates	Learning Plan
Arc 1	In social studies, students will identify key vocabulary for talking about identity. In literacy, students will draw upon identity work to learn about themselves as readers and writers. Learning Activities:

Literacy	Social Studies
• Model and write "I Am . . ." poem (preassessment). • Write initial personal narrative story (preassessment). • Unpack Narrative Writing Checklist, identifying strengths and goals for personal narrative writing. • Begin revising personal narratives by discussing beginning, middle, and end.	• Pose initial question: What makes you who you are? Students share thoughts on sticky notes to support co-construction of identity vocabulary. • Read All Are Welcome by Alexandra Penfold and Suzanne Kaufman (2018) and create Circle Map (Hyerle, 2015) to brainstorm identity words

(Continued)

Dates	Learning Plan	
	Literacy	**Social Studies**

		• Introduce Thinking Journals
		
		   ○ See-Think-Wonder (Ritchhart et al., 2011)
		
		   ○ I used to. . . . Now I . . . (Ritchhart et al., 2011)
		
		• Sort identity words from Circle Map to identify categories for identity (ie., gender, sexual orientation, race/ethnicity) using iCardSort. Create a list of "group identities."
		
		• Goal-Setting Activity: What are your personal goals this year?

Arc 2	Students will unpack their identities, using key vocabulary from Week 1, resulting in additions to Identity Maps. In literacy, they will explore their lives as readers and continue writing personal narratives, learning how to edit and revise through peer feedback. Learning Activities	
	Literacy	**Social Studies**

	• Revise personal narratives by modeling how to add dialogue and sensory details.
	
	• Model peer conferencing for student-to-student feedback on personal narratives.
	
	• Edit personal narratives for paragraphing and indentation; introduce editing checklist.
	
	• Collect work sample of personal narratives for self-assessment with checklist.
		• Scaffold identifying parts of identities (group identities, roles, family culture, important stories, etc.) and add to Identity Popplets, spread across multiple lessons.
		
		   ○ Lesson 1: Traits vs. Roles
		
		   ○ Lesson 2: Group Identities
		
		   ○ Lesson 3: Important Moments and Family History/Culture

Dates	Learning Plan

	Literacy	Social Studies

	• Begin "My Reading Timeline" project, where students create a timeline of their reading life, sharing favorite books and important moments in their history as readers.	• Send Home Family Culture Survey (Home Connection) where students choose questions to interview family members; bring notes back to school to include in Identity Popplets.
		
		• Read alouds to continue to support discussions about identity, including
		   ○ <u>Fly Away Home</u>
		   ○ <u>King and King</u>
		   ○ <u>The Lotus Seed</u>
		   ○ <u>Hidden Figures</u>
		• Thinking Journals
		   ○ How has your thinking about identity changed?
		   ○ What makes you who you are?

Arc 3	Students will compare and contrast identities with classmates, developing an appreciation for similarities and differences between identities. In literacy, students will begin to reflect on their first personal narrative so they can articulate their strengths and challenges as writers. Learning Activities

	Literacy	Social Studies
	• What do strong readers and writers do? Create a Circle Map to be added to as the year progresses. • Reflect on first personal narrative and set goals for a new narrative using self-reflection and Narrative Writing Checklist.	• Create Double Bubble Maps, scaffolded and supported across multiple days. • Create an "identity mural" that illustrates important pieces of identity both symbolically and literally, to hand with final "I Am . . ." Poem.

(Continued)

Dates	Learning Plan	
	Literacy	**Social Studies**

	• Model starting a second personal narrative using reflection and Narrative Writing Checklist.
	
	• Model "revising as you go," using Lift a Line strategy (Buckner, 2005).
	
	• Share reading timelines with small groups; record a retelling of the reading timeline on Seesaw.
		• Thinking Journals
		
		  o How has your thinking about identity changed?
		
		  o What makes you who you are?

Arc 4	Students will demonstrate how their understanding of identity has changed over the course of the unit. Students will use the Reading Timeline project and Personal Narratives to discuss how they want to grow as readers and writers. Learning Activities	
	Literacy	**Social Studies**
	• Finish editing and revising personal narratives to prepare for publishing party. • Celebrate writing progress with publishing party, using Narrative Writing Checklist and reflection activity to compare initial narrative to new narrative. • Goal-Setting Activity: What are your strengths and challenges as a reader and writer? Use personal narratives and reading timeline as a provocation for future goals.	• Complete identity murals and back them for hanging. • Complete Final "I Am . . ." poems. • Put finishing touches on Bubble Maps and Double Bubble Maps. • Compare "I Am . . ." poems to analyze how thinking about identity has changed. • Final Thinking Journal Entry How has your thinking changed about identity? (I used to think . . . Now I think . . .)

You can find this unit with links to resources for specific lessons on my website.
http://www.paulemerich.com/resources *(Adapted from Wiggins and McTighe, 2005).*

This initial learning experience where we explored Penfold and Kaufman's book was only an introduction into identity, and subsequent lessons were intended to deepen their understanding. In a later lesson, students would categorize these identity words using iCardSort, a digital card sorting app, helping us come up with broad indicators for identity like race/ethnicity, gender, clothing, age, ability, and more, ultimately setting them up with the vocabulary to conduct a self-study of identity.

In Sara Ahmed's book, *Being the Change* (2018), she suggests taking a very similar approach to starting the year by talking about identity, offering a list of books to choose from. She also introduces **identity webs** as an activity that students can complete to learn more about themselves and others. While I don't follow Ahmed's process explicitly, I do something quite similar, instead incorporating *Thinking Maps* into our identity study.

In case you're unfamiliar, *Thinking Maps* are a set of metacognitive tools that allow students to organize their thinking (Hyerle, 1995). They use eight foundational thinking maps that can be applied to nearly any context. While the Circle Map from the first lesson offers a structure for *brainstorming*, Bubble Maps provide a structure for *describing*. When planning for humanized instruction from a distance, we must break down barriers between disciplines. We can, in fact, teach identity, metacognitive, and executive functioning learning objectives simultaneously. Finding these opportunities for cross-disciplinary learning makes teaching more embodied and sustainable.

When conducting identity studies with my students, I lead by modeling. In order for students to learn how to talk about their identities, they must see adults do it first. I make my identity map along with them, allowing me to not only model, but also scaffold the process of naming parts of their identities. When I don't scaffold this process for my students, their maps tend to become unwieldy and hard to understand. They tend to focus on what I call roles or interests, adding words like dancer, artist, baseball player, or gamer to their maps. These words are important, don't get me wrong, but so are group identities, significant moments or stories from their lives, traits, and their family history.

Even when we're in person, I like to use Popplet for this—but it's great for distance learning, too. Popplet is a child-friendly concept mapping tool that allows students to create and connect "popples." The popples form the bubbles in the Bubble Map (see Figure 5.3), and the color-coding tool can be used to help students differentiate between the different parts of their identities: purple represents group identities; gray represents family history; green represents significant stories from their lives; blue represents "traits" (i.e., adjectives that describe their personalities); and orange represents the roles they play in their lives. The color-coding and categorization also serve as a great assessment. If students have a disproportionate amount of one color, it allows me to see if they need help building vocabulary in one area of identity or another.

Figure 5.3: Mr. France's Identity Popplet

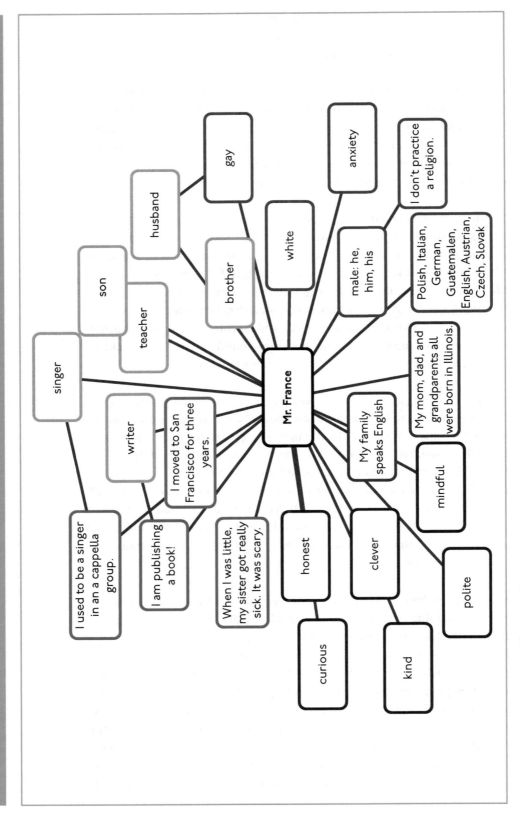

The reality is that you could categorize the maps in any way you want. The categories I've provided made sense to me and to my students, but there are lots of ways to categorize identity. Some teachers categorize identities based on visible (i.e., race/ethnicity, physical disability) or invisible (i.e., gender, religion, sexuality), while others might categorize identities based on dominant or marginalized identities, as Liz Kleinrock of @TeachandTransform has done. The possibilities are truly endless. If it feels developmentally appropriate for your group of students, categorizing identities in multiple different ways could be an excellent exercise for mindfulness and mental dexterity.

STORYTELLING

Being an independent learner not only entails being able to articulate pieces of your identity, it also entails learning how to tell your story. We can tell our stories from anywhere—both in person and through a screen.

Chimamanda Ngozi Adichie, internationally recognized author of short stories and novels, shares the "Danger of a Single Story" in her now famous TED talk, which has garnered over 22 million views on the TED website alone. In it, she shares her experiences being on the receiving end of the stereotypes generated from what she calls "single stories," as well as her experiences perpetuating the single story when meeting and learning about others.

"Stories matter," she says. "Many stories matter. Stories have been used to dispossess and to malign, but stories can also be used to empower and to humanize. Stories can break the dignity of a people, but stories can also repair that broken dignity."

All students who come into our classrooms, but especially those with marginalized identities, are subject to the stereotypes that single-story thinking brings upon them. These single stories reinforce problematic narratives, including but not limited to the gender binary, racial stereotypes, classist preconceptions about students from working-class or low-income families, and the deficit-based thinking that pervades the lives of neurodivergent students and students with disabilities. By holding space for students to tell their stories, we take a step toward disrupting and mitigating the dangerous implications of the "single story."

We can't possibly expect to be able to tell our students' stories for them. For white teachers like me, that would inevitably mean whitewashing stories of our Students of Color, and for straight, cisgender teachers, that could even entail telling stories through a heteronormative or binary lens. When we allow students to tell stories on their own terms and in their own ways, we dismantle the mechanisms that whitewash, straight-wash, or cis-wash our students' stories. We grant them the opportunity to stand on their own two feet and tell their stories, free of bias and discrimination.

Patriarchal, white supremacist thinking tells us that we have to departmentalize our content and siphon off subjects into distinct parts of the day. But when we take a humanized and embodied approach to any sort of learning, we see that we actually do our students a greater service by breaking down these walls and helping them see the connections between different content areas. By making the connections between subject areas concrete, we bolster independence and add purpose to learning. That's why I prefer to plan in a style where all content areas are united by a single essential question. In the beginning of the year, the perfect essential question is this: *What makes you who you are?* Even if your school day is broken up into distinct subjects (i.e., reading, writing, math, science, social studies), like so many schools require, you can still explore this question in all of these different contexts, while still adhering to your school's guidelines for content delivery:

- Who are you as a reader?

- Who are you as a writer?

- Who are you as a mathematician and scientist?

- What are the similarities and differences between your identities in each of these areas?

In reading workshop, you can talk about reading habits, personal reading goals, and the types of books that students like to read. In math workshop and science, students can study all sorts of scientists, centering People of Color, women, and LGBTQ+ figures in STEM. And in writing, students can write personal narratives or short stories about important moments in their lives, all the while infusing core academic skills that we know students need for success in future grades and their adult lives.

Storytelling is one of the ways that I come out to my students each year. For a couple of years now, I have used our first unit on personal narratives (which ties very nicely into the unit on identity from Figure 4.3) to write my own, including my partner David, in my stories.

Before David and I were married, I remember writing a story called "Goliath," about riding a rollercoaster at an amusement park the summer prior to school starting. Naturally, David was there, and because he was a critical character in my story, I mentioned him.

We were in the very front car. I wrote. *I looked over at David who had his eyes closed. David gets very scared on rollercoasters.*

"Who's David?" one of the students blurted out.

"Oh!" I replied knowingly. "I probably should clarify who my other character is."

I inserted a carrot and wrote *my partner*.

"What's a partner?" another one blurted out.

Needless to say, we were still working on raising our hands before speaking.

"Well," I began thoughtfully and intentionally, "a partner is kind of like how two parents are together—kind of like moms and dads. It's two people who really love each other who share their lives and do things together."

There was a slight pause, as I'm sure this was a slightly new idea for some of them.

"Thank you so much for asking that," I replied. "It's important to consider our audience when we write, and we need to make sure we clarify who our characters are. But make sure to raise your hand next time."

I winked. And we moved on.

Later on in the next week, when we were doing the aforementioned identity maps, I used it as an opportunity to share that one of the words I use to describe myself is *gay*.

"Wait," one student asked, "you're gay?"

I looked at him, somewhat surprised.

"Yea," I said. "I told you about my partner, David, remember?"

"Oh!" he replied. "Now I remember."

While I can't be sure exactly what was going on in that child's mind, I can imagine that they had only heard the word "gay" mentioned in a negative or pejorative context, and this was one of the first (or maybe even only) times that he had heard someone self-identify as such, slowly chipping away at the heteronormative bias that had captured his mind.

I now feel much more comfortable doing this with my students. I off-handedly mention David, which serves to normalize my sexuality and relationship with my husband. But it's important to recognize that my situation brings me a great deal of privilege. LGBTQ+ teachers who are non-partnered or bisexual often have their identities erased in schools. When their relationships pass as heteronormative or if they are non-partnered, there are fewer opportunities to actually *share* about their sexual orientation or gender identity in a way that does not trigger uncomfortable or unsafe responses in other adults. As a result, it's our jobs when we have cisgender privilege or the privilege that comes from an accepted sexual identity that we bring marginalized LGBTQ+ identities into the classroom in any way possible. People's lives very literally depend on it.

INFUSING IDENTITY INTO EVERYTHING YOU TEACH

Starting the year with a unit on identity opens up innumerous possibilities for the remainder of the year. Because students have been exposed to all of the vocabulary related to identity, I am able to refer to it in other parts of the curriculum and in everyday conversations.

About a month into distance learning this past spring, I noticed my students were using the chat function quite a bit in Google Meet. To be honest, the chats were getting out of hand, and so we were due for a conversation about our agreements and how to use the chats and emojis responsibly. But I hadn't anticipated the conversation about race that came up.

I oftentimes used the "thumbs up" and "thumbs down" emojis as a quick check-in. As I mentioned in Chapter 1, I don't think it's appropriate to require kids to keep their cameras on. It's invasive and intrusive. The emoji check-ins served as a great way to make sure kids were at the very least processing what they were hearing, but also gave me some information about who I needed to check in with after the minilessons had concluded.

But I began to notice that some of my white students were using emojis meant for People of Color.

I contemplated how I might go about having a conversation about this. I knew that I needed to talk to them about it, because it was a clear sign of appropriation, but I wanted to do it in a way that called them in, instead of calling them out. I wondered if, perhaps, I should have had the conversation with only my white students, but I ultimately decided against that. Shrouding these conversations in secrecy only creates anxiety about topics like cultural appropriation. Plus, it was a community space, and the appropriation was occurring in that community space. As a result, it made sense to address it in that same community space.

The following day, I prepared a slide (Figure 5.4) with an image of all five emoji skin tones, with the question: What is the *impact* of using emojis of color when you're white?

APPROPRIATE EMOJI USE

What is the **impact** of using emojis of color when you're white?

- It could send a message you don't want it to send.
- It could make people feel like you're making fun of them.
- It might look like you are taking on someone else's identity when it's not yours to take.

Why did they create different color emojis?

- They wanted people to be able to show their skin color and show their identity.
- Maybe some people of color didn't like that they had to use one that isn't their color.
- Maybe people didn't feel comfortable using something that didn't relate to them.
- **Representation** matters in all places.

I can't be sure whether or not they knew it was wrong prior to our conversation, but it became obvious there was an issue because we were having a class meeting about it. They threw out a number of ideas right away.

"Someone might think you're making fun of them," one student said, as I added it to the Google slide.

"Ah, yes," I replied. "That most certainly could happen. And we don't want anyone feeling that way, right?"

I want to emphasize that I didn't even speak about *intention* with them. Why? Because the intention really didn't matter. What mattered most was the impact of the behavior, and by leading with the impact of the behavior, I centered impact in our conversation.

We continued talking, and my students continued to unmute their microphones, offering ideas similar to the first, making it clear that they didn't yet understand the strong link to identity in this conversation.

"There's another reason I want to share with you," I confided in them. "Sometimes, when you use an emoji that's not the same color of your skin, it might look like you are trying to take on someone else's identity—when it's not yours to take."

The chat was pretty silent, and while it may sound strange to say, I could sense that I had their attention, even though I couldn't hear any of them and could only see half of them.

"When you take on someone else's identity, it's called 'appropriation.' Can you say that word?"

The whole class unmuted their microphones and repeated, "appropriation."

As an aside, unmuting and repeating is another great way to make sure students are engaged or processing what you're saying. When they have to repeat key vocabulary, they get practice saying the word, and you also can check in on who is with you and who may have wandered off.

"Appropriation is not a good thing, and when white people do it to People of Color, it is racist and can really hurt people's feelings. I'm wondering, why do you think they created different color emojis in the first place?"

And of course, they had lots of ideas.

"They wanted people to be able to show their skin color and show their identity," one student said. And there it was: the connection to identity.

"Absolutely," I replied. "Any other ideas?"

They listed off a few other ideas, which you can see in Figure 5.4, and after they finished sharing, I added another new vocabulary word: "representation."

"Representation matters in all places," I said. "People need to be able to show their identities, even when they're sending chats in Google Meet!"

The conversation ended positively, and after that, I did not see another inappropriately used emoji. It revealed to me the power of building a strong classroom culture that is not only able to unpack and study identity, but one that is able to have critical conversations about race, power, and privilege. Kids are capable of having these discussions, even when learning from a distance, and we need to invest our trust and faith in them so that they can learn, at a young age, that identity matters and that it pervades every corner of our society.

THE IMPACT OF IDENTITY

At the end of this past year, in what would be my last year in the classroom for the foreseeable future, I received a phone call from a parent. They had wanted to follow up about a recent conversation about academic progress, as we hadn't had enough time to finish our prior conversation. We discussed what we needed to, and then the parent closed the conversation with something quite unexpected.

I had gotten married the previous October, and I was lucky enough to be able to celebrate my wedding with the class. I was greeted one morning with a huge cluster of rainbow-themed balloons, along with a beautiful gift, and a book of "advice" on how to be a good husband to David.

"I just wanted to say thank you," she said, "for sharing so much about yourself and for celebrating your wedding with the kids this year. For [Alex], it's now just such a normal thing to him, and we're so grateful that he had you as his teacher and that he knows that now. We were actually telling him how [gay marriage] used to be illegal, and he couldn't believe it!"

It has certainly not always been an easy road for me, being faced with the conundrum of coming out to my students and their families each year. But moments like these make every moment I've struggled worth it. That child is going to grow up with a radically different perception of the world, and while heteronormativity and homophobia will still be powerful forces that will need to be continuously dismantled, he will always remember that his third-grade teacher was gay—and that there was nothing to be scared of. What's more, he will interact with countless people in the world, and while I know he won't be able to change all hearts and minds, he might be able to use his memory of me to change at least some of them.

The impact of identity work in schools transcends the relatively concrete relationships we create with our students. Our mere presence in our students' lives—coupled with our willingness to let ourselves and our identities be seen by them—creates ripple effects that will very literally change the trajectory of our world and the lives of the people who inhabit it. This work can, of course, be done in person, but it can also be done from a distance—and it's likely that the impact will reach an even further distance than the space that exists between you and your students' devices.

TIPS FOR TEACHING FROM A DISTANCE, CHAPTER 5

- Study identity. It's never too late to start.

- Infuse identity into everything that you teach.

- Plan for identity studies with intention. Leverage backward design and the Five-Question Planning Template.

- Make space for storytelling in your classroom.

- Model unpacking identity by sharing yourself with your students.

CHAPTER SIX

REDEFINING STUDENT SUCCESS

A hallmark of differentiated instruction is an educator's ability to "meet students where they are." This phrase has become relatively commonplace in modern classrooms, so much so that it has become a gold standard of quality teaching. But we can't meet students where they are if we don't have a way to find out where exactly that place is. Humanized assessment practices offer educators the opportunity to meet students there. When assessment is *humanized*, it centers the child's humanity, allowing educators to reframe assessment not as a means for categorizing or controlling students, but instead as a provocation—a data point that allows us to be curious about students.

With good reason, educators and parents alike tense up when they hear the word "assessment." For decades now, standardized assessments have been weaponized in schools, further marginalizing neurodivergent students, Students of Color, and multilingual learners. The standardized assessments that have become so commonplace in schools are a product of an industrial age vision of schools as sorting factories. Much in the way that proponents of the pseudoscience of eugenics aimed to create barriers to the success of immigrants, these norm-referenced tests serve to perpetuate long standing structural inequities in our society. They are of little value to educators as an indicator of student potential or growth, are culturally biased, and reify white supremacist values. Moreover, they can have long-term, damaging effects on students—particularly those who represent historically marginalized groups. While many teachers have been conditioned to live and breathe by such metrics, there is a growing awareness that we must repurpose classroom assessment, making it a tool for knowing students as human beings, paving a path to independence and student liberation.

The word "assessment" comes from the Latin *assessus*, meaning "a sitting by." What a fascinating and enlightening reframe, to think of assessment as "sitting by" a child to know, understand, and partner with them, as opposed of "standing over, categorizing, or controlling" them. All assessment should be as such: It should be a partnership, a conversation, and a means for guiding students from a reasonable distance.

When we reframe assessment as "sitting by" instead of "standing over," it becomes immediately clear that effective feedback practices lie at the heart of effective humanized assessment. In the next chapter, we'll discuss complex instruction and the power of balancing whole-group, small-group, and individualized instruction. Part of the reason we should strive to balance these three dimensions of instruction is because we want to maximize the time we have to offer verbal feedback in small groups or individualized conferences. Of course, this doesn't mean that we cannot use formal means of assessment and provide written feedback, as well. Formal paper-and-pencil assessments are helpful in capturing what students know and are able to do.

It's not necessarily the presence of assessment that dehumanizes students, schools, and the education system as a whole. It is, instead, the *why*, the *what*, and *how* we are assessing that is doing so. As a result, we must use this moment in time as an opportunity to dismantle oppressive assessment practices and reconfigure them in the image of an ever-diversifying group of learners. We must identify a clear cycle for assessment that makes it ongoing and informative, and we must make our students partners in this cycle for assessment, so that we center their experiences and their humanity, meanwhile avoiding categorizing, controlling, or institutionalizing them.

THE *WHY*

I start every year with the same conversation. Within the first week or two of school, I begin my usual routine of conducting beginning-of-year assessments. These might take the form of an independent writing task, some one-on-one reading time with me, or perhaps even a paper-and-pencil math assessment, confined to the Established Goals I've identified for the first unit of math.

 "Do you know why we do assessments at school?" I ask my students.

The conversation usually goes the same way every year.

"To find out if we're good or bad at something?" one student will say.

"To find out what group we're going to be in for reading," another will posit.

"To me," I reply, "it's not about being 'good' or 'bad' at something. I use assessments for a different reason: I want to see what I need to teach you all."

Generally speaking, they're not convinced that I actually mean this, so I continue on.

"Think of it like this," I'll say. "If I don't give you an assessment of some sort, then I'm not going to know if what I'm teaching you is too easy, too hard, or just right for you. An assessment gives you an opportunity to tell me that."

Framing assessment in this manner creates a conversation between teachers and students. It helps them see that assessment is actually a tool for getting to know them as learners, as opposed to a tool for categorizing them into "good" and "bad" readers, writers, mathematicians, and human beings. Moreover, this starts an on-going conversation about assessment, helping students see that assessments are not just to inform future learning, assessments can also be learning tools that help students get to know *themselves* better, cultivating self-awareness and self-advocacy skills in the process (Gottlieb, 2016).

This conversation must be ongoing; it must be a part of the cultural fabric of your classroom. No matter how humanized your assessment practices are, you must remember that our students will grow up and continue to live in a white supremacist and patriarchal society that values categorization and social control. As a result, I continue having this conversation repetitively over the course of the entire year, reminding students that assessments are there to help me see what to teach them next, even if it means I have to review something with them.

Aligning on the *why* behind assessment also helps reframe conversations around independence, helping my students understand that their assessments must be completed independently—without the help of a peer or teacher. If they aren't, the assessments won't actually be telling me what *they* know and are able to do.

"Here's the thing," I'll tell them. "If you work with a buddy on this assessment, it's going to tell me what you and your buddy can do *together*. If you copy from a buddy, it's going to tell me what *your buddy* knows and is able to do—not you. Remember, assessments are there to help me see what to teach *you* next, and so if you collaborate on assessments when you're not supposed to, you're giving me information that isn't going to help me help you."

That said, there are times where assessment can and should be collaborative; there are times where collaborative assessment on group projects is actually desirable and growth oriented. We can draw these boundaries with our students simply by communicating with them. I experienced this during remote learning when my students were participating in their animal research clubs, inspired by Lucy Calkins Units of Study (Calkins & Tolan, 2015). These were group projects by design, providing students much needed opportunities to collaborate and socialize during distance learning, but also allowing them to learn collaboratively, leveraging each other's strengths and the benefits of peer modeling in the process. They documented their weekly research on Seesaw, along with self-reflections in relation to our checklists.

Truth be told, I don't have a lot of issues with "copying" or "cheating" in my classrooms. Not only do I construct my assessments in a manner that is open-ended and requires critical thought, I am confident that the rationale and culture I set up around assessment disincentivizes any sort of copying or academic dishonesty.

The moment we make assessment high-stakes, we increase the likelihood that students will engage in dishonest behaviors. Desperation would make any reasonable human being break the rules, and when we put pressure on our students by making assessments high stakes, we create that desperation in them. Conversely, when we take this pressure off of students and continuously remind them that the purpose of assessment is *communication*, we incentivize entirely different behaviors.

"Mr. France," some students will inevitably say to me in the middle of an assessment, "I really just don't get it."

"That's okay," I might say in reply. "Do me a favor, though. Will you write me a note about what you don't understand or what is confusing? Try to find a word you don't know or a phrase that's troubling you."

This reinforces the idea that assessment truly is about communication. By writing me a note, students are telling me, very clearly, what they know, what they don't know, and what I need to teach them next. Their note serves as a concrete reminder of that when they look back at it later, as well as an artifact for their portfolios that helps their parents see where they're struggling. While I always challenge my students to be entirely independent on assessments, there are some instances when I do find it necessary to intervene and assist.

"Does it make more sense now?" I'll ask after intervening and clarifying.

"It does!" students will say in reply if my explanation was sufficient. "Thanks for the help."

"I'm just going to write a little note on your assessment to remind you that I helped with this question," I add. "That way, when you're doing your reflection afterward, you can reflect on this obstacle and remember that we did it together."

This, once again, normalizes assessment, reinforcing the idea that assessment is merely a documentation of learning and that reflection is a critical part of an assessment cycle. Once we've begun clarifying the purpose of assessment, we can engage our students in understanding another component of assessment. We can help them identify *what* we're assessing.

THE *WHAT*

Similar to the word "assessment," many progressive educators pause when they hear the words "standard" and "standardize." Again, this is warranted, as standards, too, have been weaponized against marginalized students, operating in opposition to educational equity. When humanizing assessment and using standards equitably, they must merely serve as a guide—a flexible structure that provides common language for what we hope students learn

Dr. Gholdy Muhammad, associate professor at George State University provides a four-layer equity framework for culturally and historically responsive literacy (HRL) in her book *Cultivating Genius* (2020). When lesson planning, she encourages educators to use each of the four layers to identify learning objectives. The four layers are as follows: Identity, Skills, Intellect, and Criticality. She, too, encourages teachers to center humanity when identifying learning objectives, and by expanding the confines of what we identify as learning objectives, Dr. Muhammad does just that. In the previous chapters, we discussed the importance of incorporating identity objectives into academic instruction. Muhammad layers upon Identity objectives with a Skills layer, much like the typical academic skills or standards you might expect. Her third layer, Intellect, relates to the essential questions within backward design, written to broaden the context in which students learn. And finally, her fourth layer, Criticality, refers to learning objectives that teach about power, privilege, equity, and social justice, in an effort to dismantle oppressive structures and teach for social change.

So are these standards? Is Dr. Muhammad encouraging us to identify standards within her four-layer equity framework? And if so, is this identification of standards inequitable?

Muhammad refers to them as "learning pursuits," but when all is said and done, naming what we want students to know and be able to do simply adds clarity and precision to our practice for ourselves, our students, and their parents, whether we call them standards, learning goals, or competencies. Identifying clear learning objectives, skills, or standards is also an equitable practice. By clarifying what we want students to know and be able to do, we are communicating that we will be holding all students to a high standard, even if it means adjusting the scaffolds students require to reach these standards. Similar to socioemotional learning, this all operates under the assumption that teachers are doing anti-bias and anti-racist work in conjunction with using standards in their classrooms. Doing so will ensure they are not weaponized against marginalized students.

For some of us, our schools have done the hard work of choosing sets of standards off of which we must build assessments and learning experiences. For others, however, this may not be the case. Some schools begin by choosing instructional resources, as opposed to starting with establishing learning goals for each grade. I don't recommend this because it engenders mindlessness in our teaching. By centering or overrelying on a curriculum manual for teaching and assessment, teachers are incentivized to think far less critically about *what* they're teaching and *why* they're teaching it. It cultivates anxiety when they deviate from the curriculum manual, ultimately chipping away at teacher autonomy and prioritizing work completion over meaningful learning. In fact, one of the strengths of prioritizing learning goals over content coverage or curriculum "completion" is that we can focus on the learning and cut out unnecessary lessons when we're short on time or other resources. It also helps us personalize learning experiences, removing unnecessary scaffolds or activities when our students require varied learning paths, much like Jo from Chapter 4. I suggest using the following resources to inform *what* you'll be teaching and assessing.

- The Teaching Tolerance Framework (2019) advises teachers on skills related to identity, diversity, justice, and action. These skills are clumped into developmental ranges, flexible for diverse groups of learners, but firm enough to provide structure to your teaching and advise you on what's developmentally appropriate for your grade level.

- Common Core (2020), C3 Framework (National Council for the Social Studies, 2017), and the Next Generation Science Standards (NGSS; 2020) are all cut from the same cloth. They take a similar competency-based approach to teaching and learning, where they unpack process and even offer opportunities for interdisciplinary learning, linking science and social studies concepts to core literacy and mathematics skills.

- Yardsticks (Wood, 2007) and CASEL (2020) offer educators insight into social, emotional, cognitive, and other developmental milestones. While these are "assessed" a bit differently than academic skills might be, they may inform your approach to distance learning and allow you to get to the root of challenges with your distance learning approach.

When using any sort of standard set, we *must* remember that many of them reflect white supremacist and/or patriarchal values. As a result, we must be mindful pedagogues who think of sets of standards as flexible frameworks that promote learning through common language. It's possible, as I've experienced before, that a given standard or competency may not be right for your class or an individual child. If, perhaps, you notice persistent obstacles with a given standard or set of standards, it's entirely possible that it's not the right fit for your school or your community. As a result, educators should be trusted to take a needs-based approach when it comes to choosing standards and make changes as they see fit.

For example, I've worked with countless students who struggle with risk-taking and vulnerability. I've seen this challenge since the very beginning of my career, and as a result, it has become a standard of sorts in my classroom. If Dr. Muhammad were to categorize it, I expect it might go in the *Intellect* category, fitting neatly in with socioemotional competencies or learning habits. Risk-taking is not explicitly stated as a skill or standard in most curricula and, again, keep in mind that it is somewhat antithetical to striving for perfectionism—one of the characteristics of white supremacist thinking. However, the ability to tolerate uncertainty and to simply *try* something is critical to building independent learning habits in our students. Without explicitly teaching students how to take risks, we reinforce dependent learning habits, and we limit opportunities for students to experience the dissonance, frustration, and sense of accomplishment that come from taking risks.

Taking risks and making mistakes is critical to distance learning, and if you haven't already done so, I recommend using morning meetings or perhaps even synchronous learning blocks to conduct whole lessons on what it looks like to take risks and make mistakes. Figure 6.1 gives just one example of a lesson you could teach, using the book *The Girl Who Never Made Mistakes* (Pett & Rubenstein, 2011).

Question 1: What do I hope students will leave knowing or being able to do?

Students will be able to identify the importance of making mistakes and discuss the negative consequences of not making mistakes.

Question 2: How will I know if students understand this?

Before the read aloud, I will channel students' background knowledge by talking about making mistakes. I will connect mistake making to other lessons on emotional literacy, asking them: How do you feel when you take a risk or make a mistake? I will collect ideas in a Circle Map on the easel to document our class's thinking.

Question 3: What instructional resource will I use to provoke curiosity and discussion?

The Girl Who Never Made Mistakes by Mark Pett and Gary Rubenstein (2011)

Question 4: How will I facilitate the discussion?

I will stop at key points throughout the book to reflect on the characters and their choices, tying the discussion into our study of character traits:

- How are Beatrice and her brother different? How are they similar?
- Why do you think Carl loves to make mistakes but Beatrice doesn't?
- What happens to Beatrice when she almost made a mistake? How did that impact her heart and her mind?
- What did Beatrice learn at the end of the story? What helped her learn this?
- How did making a mistake help Beatrice?

Question 5: How will we reflect on this discussion?

Students will reflect on this read aloud in their thinking journals by responding to the question: Why is it important to make mistakes? They may use the following sentence frames as scaffolds for their journaling, or abandon the scaffolds if they have a different idea:

- It's important to make mistakes because _____
- If I never made any mistakes, then _____
- When I make mistakes, I feel _____
- Next time, I make a mistake, I will _____
- In the story, Beatrice never makes mistakes. This was _____ because _____

Humanized assessment is built on a needs-based and human-centered approach to identifying learning objectives, standards, or skills. A critical part of building independence in students is identifying the barriers they are experiencing and teaching to those. So often, student barriers are less related to the content itself, and more about ancillary competencies related to socioemotional or cognitive skills. So often, strengths and barriers can be found within students' humanity.

This lesson on making mistakes and other lessons I teach on risk-taking and vulnerability did not come about simply because I decided I wanted to teach them; they came about because I noticed that my students needed them. I observed them and noticed that their collective tendency to avoid risks and strive for perfection was getting in the way of success in school. I also now know that striving for such perfectionism is a characteristic of white supremacy (Jones & Okun, 2001), and, consequently, something that we must work to dismantle.

No matter in what form, teaching from a distance and teaching for independence means that we must continuously observe our students, and pivot our teaching based on their needs as human beings. As we engage in virtual learning, and as we return to in-person learning, we will continuously discover new strengths and challenges within our students. As teachers, we must be empowered to identify and teach to these if we want our students to succeed as independent learners who learn at a distance from their teachers.

THE *HOW*

Always start with the *why* and the *what* of assessment. Our *why* for assessment will inevitably impact *what* we assess, and the combination of these will impact *how* we assess. This is known as Campbell's Law. Campbell's Law tells us that "the more any quantitative social indicators is used for social decision-making, the more subject it will be to corruption pressures and the more apt it will be to distort and corrupt the social processes it is intended to monitor" (Campbell, 1979). For instance, if we use multiple-choice assessments in our classrooms, it is likely we will teach in a manner that mirrors a traditional multiple-choice assessment. On the contrary, if we qualitatively assess student progress through journaling prompts, small-group work, and individualized conferences, all of which are contextualized by real-world and authentic learning experiences, we will be more likely to tap into the humanity of learning and our students' journeys as human beings. Knowing that Campbell's Law will impact our practice no matter what we do, we should leverage it in a way that works in our students' favor.

Assessing virtually is undoubtedly more challenging than assessing in the classroom. That said, assessing should, in many ways, always happen at a distance. If we intervene or offer too much assistance when assessing—that is, if we don't sit back and observe students as they stand on their own two feet—then a child's work will be less so an indicator of what *they* can do, and more so an indicator of what they can accomplish with adult assistance. That won't provide you the information you need to help them step into their independence and liberate themselves.

While the following assessment strategies are intended to help you assess virtually through distance teaching, these could very well transform your assessment practices, humanizing assessment and empowering your students from no matter where you're teaching.

PERIODIC DIGITAL FORMATIVE ASSESSMENTS

Distance learning feels more challenging to teachers due to the amount of student work that tends to be generated in the process. If you're a general education classroom teacher like me, teaching multiple subjects each day to twenty or more students, you know that student work adds up quickly. But even if you're a middle- or high-school teacher who teaches the same lesson multiple times over the course of a day, the mere number of students you have also means that student work will add up just as quickly.

In Chapter 4, we talked about sustainable planning, reframing the conversation from planning only in terms of daily lessons to planning in terms of arcs instead. Doing so allows you to plan formative assessment checkpoints, where you can collect one work sample that encompasses a week's worth of lessons, or perhaps even more. Grading every single assignment or task students generate is not only unsustainable, it's also wholly unnecessary. Oftentimes, these assignments are completed in collaboration with peers or with the help of an adult, giving us little to no information on what the child can actually complete on their own. Let's look at an example.

In my third-grade class this past spring, my final unit in math encompassed the following Common Core skills, listed in the "Established Goals" section of my unit design document.

CCSS.MATH.CONTENT.3.G.A.1

Understand that shapes in different categories (e.g., rhombuses, rectangles, and others) may share attributes (e.g., having four sides), and that the shared attributes can define a larger category (e.g., quadrilaterals). Recognize rhombuses, rectangles, and squares as examples of quadrilaterals, and draw examples of quadrilaterals that do not belong to any of these subcategories.

CCSS.MATH.CONTENT.3.MD.C.6

Measure areas by counting unit squares (square cm, square m, square in., square ft, and improvised units).

CCSS.MATH.CONTENT.3.MD.C.7

Relate area to the operations of multiplication and addition.

CCSS.MATH.CONTENT.3.MD.D.8

Solve real-world and mathematical problems involving perimeters of polygons, including finding the perimeter given the side lengths, finding an unknown side length, and exhibiting rectangles with the same perimeter and different areas or with the same area and different perimeters.

I leverage complex instruction when teaching math, meaning that I use open-ended tasks and discourse as the main source of my instruction. Students attempt the tasks on their own and then engage in a class discussion about various methods, in an effort to help students access and use more sophisticated methods as they progress.

The first couple of weeks of this unit were dedicated to categorizing shapes based on attributes. I used Seesaw to create activities that allowed students to sort shapes within the app, discussing various attributes of shapes along the way, including the number of sides, as well as the presence of right angles, parallel lines, equal or unequal sides. In fact, each task was relatively similar to the previous one, reinforcing classification, which Dr. Muhammad might call an intellectual skill. *Classifying* is a cognitive task that is critical to independent learning. By classifying shapes, we build deductive reasoning skills in students, allowing them to use universal characteristics within a given category to build vocabulary around shape attributes.

I could have formally assessed each of these tasks, as each of my students had completed them and submitted them in Seesaw. But that would have taken me hours each day, given the complexity of the work and the number of slides present within each Seesaw activity. Providing that amount of feedback was simply unsustainable. That said, I did look through their work each day, searching for glaring misconceptions or trends within the class. For instance, within this first week, I noticed students categorizing shapes based on colors. They grouped them by "hot colors" (red, orange, and yellow) and "cool colors" (green, blue, and purple) drawing upon their knowledge of colors from art class.

"I noticed that many of you grouped the shapes by color yesterday," I told them as we began the lesson. "But I want to review the definition of the word *attribute*. Does anyone remember what it means?"

One of the students replied and alluded to the fact that an attribute is a fixed characteristic of a shape.

"If I change the color of a square, is it still a square?" I questioned.

The obvious answer was yes, and with that simple review, based on an observable and pervasive misconception in my students' work, I was able to pivot midweek and address that misconception directly. Notice that this didn't require hours of laborious "grading" and endless comments on their work. It required mindfully reviewing their submissions from the day prior, and identifying major misconceptions and trends to address in whole-group instruction.

I very intentionally choose moments to formally assess student progress in relation to grade-level standards when I feel students have had ample opportunities for interpersonal feedback, exploration, and reflection on what they've learned. After multiple lessons, ranging from several days to perhaps even two full weeks of instruction, it makes sense to collect a formal assessment, independently completed by students. In the case of shape attributes, I created an assessment that mirrored the tasks they had completed in the prior week's math lessons, requiring them to sort shapes based on attributes and explain their thinking. It wasn't a multiple-choice or fill-in-the-blank assessment that limited their ability to communicate the nuances of their thinking; it was, instead, a sorting task with multiple possibilities, in which they had to explain their thinking with clarity and precision. Collecting this assessment at the conclusion of the learning arc on shape attributes made assessing my students sustainable, meanwhile giving me valuable formative data for small-group work or interventions during my office hours.

SMALL-GROUP AND ONE-ON-ONE CONFERENCES

No, I didn't just leave my students to fend for themselves in between formal formative assessments. Doing so would have been a disservice to them. Doing so would center work completion and decenter collaborative, discussion-based learning.

As we discussed in Chapter 2, I leverage the workshop model for both in-person learning and virtual distance learning. Doing so shortens my whole-group minilessons, while still allowing for valuable points of convergence and connectedness with the whole class. By maximizing time for small-group check-ins and one-on-one conferences, I am able to provide a great deal of interpersonal feedback that I know powers learning in my classroom. And of course, in order to be able to provide this feedback, I need to conduct in-the-moment anecdotal assessments of their work, similarly allowing me to uncover glaring misconceptions or gain insight into classwide trends.

To make this sustainable, I used Google Hangouts to create pods of students that I would "speed dial" once the workshop portion of the synchronous block began. Sometimes, these groupings were established based on academic need, while in other situations, these groups were formed heterogeneously, simply to make the process of reaching out to students more efficient. While I would be speaking with one student, the other students would mute their mics, continuing to work on their task(s) for the day. At other times, having a small group allowed for a more collaborative style of feedback where students offered ideas or tips for modifying or improving their peers' work. For students who needed more significant assistance, or for students who I knew felt self-conscious talking about their work in small groups, there was always the option of calling them one-on-one to provide more direct or structured guidance.

Once again, this approach to assessing students and providing feedback did not require hours of work for me after our sessions concluded; I was able to assess and provide feedback in the moment, creating a sustainable workload for me and shortening feedback loops for students. We know that these short feedback loops increase the likelihood that they will process and reflect on feedback in a timely manner, making a direct and visible impact on student learning.

CHECKING FOR UNDERSTANDING

Sometimes assessment is as simple as checking in on students to see how they are feeling about their own understanding of the content. During in-person learning, I frequently used the thumbs-up/thumbs-down technique. Students would put hands by their hearts turning their thumbs up if they were feeling confident with the content. Others would put their thumbs down if they weren't, providing me valuable information into who I should check in with first during the small-group and conferencing portion of our workshop.

During virtual distance learning, I leveraged the chat function to serve the same purpose. Students used thumbs-up and thumbs-down emojis, serving the same purpose as their real thumbs did in the classroom. In some cases, the chat served as a backchannel of sorts, allowing students to ask clarifying questions or even questions that deepened the whole class's understanding of a given topic. Interestingly, this *added* value that we didn't quite get in our in-person classroom.

Teachers are getting creative, too. One teacher on Instagram, Lauren Bakian-Aaker (@nofrillsclassroom), used simple double-sided cards as an easy way to check for understanding. One side of the card was green, and the other was red. In order for students to demonstrate their understanding, they could simply flip the card to show green or red, allowing a teacher to see very easily how much of the class felt on track, and which students felt like they needed more support.

Some students don't feel comfortable expressing their understanding (or lack thereof) in a public setting, and so I also reminded students that they could send me a private message in Google Hangouts if they didn't feel comfortable communicating in the group chat. Once again, this served the same purpose, only in a private setting.

In some instances, especially in the beginning of distance learning, I took a more formal approach to checking in on students. I created a Google Form (Figure 6.2) that I could easily link in our group chats.

Figure 6.2: Google Reflection Form

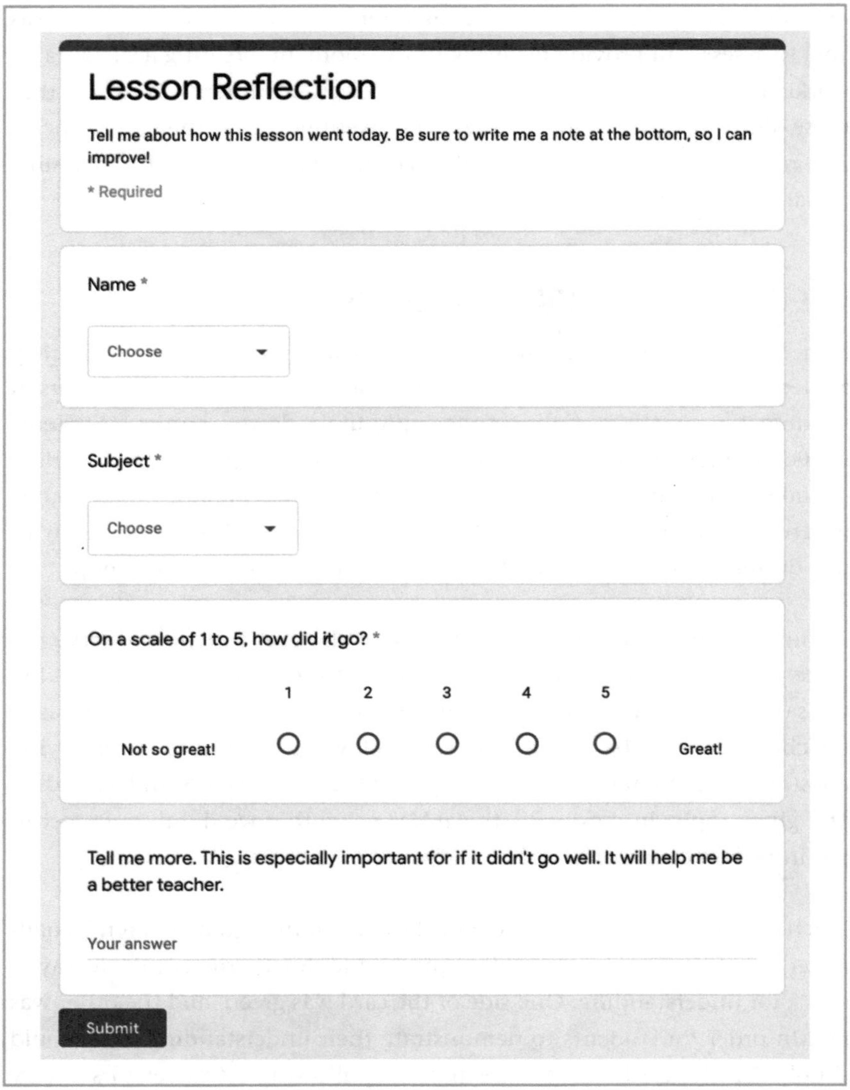

Lesson Reflection

Tell me about how this lesson went today. Be sure to write me a note at the bottom, so I can improve!

* Required

Name *

Choose

Subject *

Choose

On a scale of 1 to 5, how did it go? *

	1	2	3	4	5	
Not so great!	○	○	○	○	○	Great!

Tell me more. This is especially important for if it didn't go well. It will help me be a better teacher.

Your answer

Submit

In the form, students identified themselves and the time of day (i.e., Reading Workshop, Writing Workshop, Math Workshop), potentially providing me data on which times of day were more challenging than others. They filled out a Likert scale, rating the learning block on a scale of 1 to 5, and they also had the option of filling out an open field to tell me what was working and what wasn't. Not only did this provide an opportunity to build self-advocacy and reflection skills, it gave me great information on who was struggling and how my approach was working overall. In many ways, these data were more valuable than academic data.

SELF-REFLECTION

Providing our students with timely, actionable, and specific feedback matters a great deal. Doing so helps them see what, specifically, they need to keep doing, but also what they should change about their approach to be more effective or efficient. That said, feedback doesn't exist in a vacuum, and our students are less likely to incorporate our feedback if they don't reflect on it.

Reflection needs to happen frequently. It needs to be a part of the culture of a classroom that values independence. When teachers set routines around reflection, and when it is done repetitively, it becomes automatic. Students begin to think in a reflective manner without prompting from a teacher. They also begin to connect their efforts to their progress, understanding that the choices they make as a result of reflecting on their work ultimately contribute to incremental changes in it (Pink, 2011).

You don't need a worksheet or a journal to create a culture of reflection in your classroom. Project Zero's thinking routine "I used to . . . Now I . . ." is a great tool for both verbal and written reflection. During distance learning, educators can leverage the chat function to have students share their end-of-lesson reflections with the whole class, but this can also be done while you're maximizing your small-group learning and one-on-one conferences. In order to take a strengths-based approach in my small groups and conferences, I always begin with the strengths in their work. I do this partially to build student confidence but also because I want students to see that they can use their strengths to overcome their challenges. My compliments aren't empty words or pandering; they are tools intended to help them grow. Try some of the speaking stems from Figure 6.3 when fostering reflection with your students.

Strengths	Challenges	Next Steps
• What do you like about your work?	• What are you wondering about your work?	• What are you going to do differently next time?
• What's going well?	• What's challenging you today? Are you experiencing any obstacles?	• How has your thinking changed since the beginning of our conference?
• What are you proud of today?		
• What did you try to do differently today?	• Is there anything you're looking to change about your work?	• What's your new goal?

Within these questions lies the power of self-reflection. You'll notice that by stepping back and asking students questions, I'm challenging them to think on their own before relying on me for feedback. Oftentimes, students have a pretty good idea of what's going well and what's not. Asking them to identify that first puts the onus on them to take responsibility for their work and advocate for the help they likely already know they need. In the event that a student isn't able to identify these strengths and challenges in their own work, that may be all the assessment you need. Instead of starting with a critique of their work, pivot to make your conference or small-group minilesson about how to reflect on their work. Doing so will build a skill within them that they'll use for the rest of their lives.

CHECKLISTS AND SINGLE-POINT RUBRICS

If you notice students are struggling with reflecting, it's possible they may just not have the words to do so. This is why standards matter so much in a classroom that values independent learning. Without sharing learning goals with our students, they won't be able to articulate what they're expected to know and be able to do. As a result, they won't be able to reflect on their relative distance from the learning goal.

In the beginning of each of my units, I share with students a checklist of skills to which we continue to refer back over the course of the unit. I also use minilessons as an opportunity to build working and long-term memory by having them review and orally rehearse the skills we'll be learning aloud.

"As you're listening to me discuss the four goals for our unit, I want you to be saying them in your mind. You can show me you're saying them in your mind by spinning your pretend gear next to your head," I say as I model my finger spinning next to my head like my own gears are turning. "Now how many goals do we have for this unit?"

"Four," a handful of students say aloud.

"How many?" I ask again.

"Four!" the remainder of the class says.

"Good, there are four learning goals. The first is *identifying character traits*. Now say it in your mind."

I pause while they say the goal in their minds.

"The second goal is *identifying lessons in stories*. Say the second goal in your mind."

I continue this until I've shared all four learning goals for our unit with them. To further solidify these goals in their minds, I ask them to *rehearse* these aloud. I choose the word "rehearse" because we know that rehearsal is critical to building working memory and getting ideas stored in long-term memory. I repeat this process often in the beginning of the unit and sporadically over the course of the unit.

However, as I mentioned, I also share checklists with my students so that they may come back to this list of skills during formative assessments or conferences, listing key skills in a student-friendly format. Figure 6.4 shows an example from the fairy tales unit I mentioned in the last chapter.

Skill	Not Yet	Starting To	Got it
My fairy tale adaptation has key elements of the fairy tale I am trying to adapt.	❑	❑	❑
I introduced my story by setting the scene, introducing the characters, and identifying the problem in the story.	❑	❑	❑
I described each scene with sensory details and dialogue, helping my readers visualize my story.	❑	❑	❑
I structured my story into scenes, describing each scene in depth.	❑	❑	❑
I used transition words and phrases to move from scene to scene.	❑	❑	❑
I made new paragraphs and indented when showing a change in setting or subject.	❑	❑	❑
I showed my characters' feelings and their responses to events.	❑	❑	❑
I concluded my story with dialogue, character actions, or a lesson.	❑	❑	❑
I used what I know about prefixes, bases, and suffixes to spell challenging words.	❑	❑	❑
I punctuated dialogue with quotation marks and commas.	❑	❑	❑
I used proper capitalization and ending punctuation.	❑	❑	❑
I edited my work to make sure my words would be clear to the reader.	❑	❑	❑
I revised my work using writing strategies (i.e., lifting a line, trying ten, or rewriting scenes).	❑	❑	❑

Source: Adapted from Lucy Calkins Units of Study (2013).

Admittedly, this is a lot for kids to take in, especially for younger students. Additionally, when leveraging formative assessments, you may not want to assess every one of these objectives every single time. You may want to bite off parts of this checklist in smaller chunks, focusing on a smaller list of learning objectives each week. This necessitates a different type of checklist tool.

I used to deconstruct learning objectives to the point that I would write into my rubrics or checklists what "not yet," "starting to," and "got it" actually looked like. But the more I did that, the more frustrating assessing their work became. I realized that one child's "starting to" might look much different than another child's, and as a result, I needed a tool that offered me more flexibility. Learning is not linear, and no two learning journeys will look the same. Our tools for assessment need to reflect that.

I began using single-point rubrics (Dietz, 2000) to preserve the specificity of our checklists, meanwhile providing myself with the flexibility I needed to address various students' strengths and challenges. In a single-point rubric, the checklist item is placed in the center column, and the columns on the left and right are used for reflecting on strengths and challenges. Here's an example from the fairy tales unit:

Single-Point Rubric (Fairy Tale Structure)		
Strengths	**Fairy Tale Structure**	**Challenges/Action Steps**
	☐ My fairy tale adaptation has key elements of the fairy tale I am trying to adapt. ☐ I structured my story into scenes, describing each scene in depth like a small moment.	

This example allowed me to make my assessment sustainable and actionable by narrowing my focus and zooming in on structure in the first week of learning. The flexible nature of the single-point rubric allowed me to call out strengths related to a specific student or piece of work, as well as make some recommendations for action steps, if I see the need for any. Finally, it served as an instructional tool, allowing my students to complete the single-point rubric in Seesaw before sending it along to me with pictures of their work attached.

The single-point rubric worked for other subject areas, as well. While we were studying fairy tales in writing workshop, we were learning about research skills in reading workshop. Because I was taking a needs-based and human-centered approach, I noticed that my students' executive skills in the context of research were not strong. Because of this, I quickly whipped up a single-point rubric, identifying a few success criteria for their research notes and the research process.

Single-Point Rubric (Research Notes)		
Strengths	**Research Notes**	**Challenges/ Action Steps**
	☐ I have notes for every subtopic. ☐ I have used multiple texts for each subtopic. ☐ I have recorded the titles of the books and the authors.	

With these simple tools, formative assessment became a lot more efficient and student centered. While teaching virtually from home, efficiency really mattered; but what's great about these is that they will work well when we return to in-person learning, too. They can be easily glued in reader's and writer's notebooks, or even kept on Seesaw so they can become a part of a child's digital portfolio.

DIGITAL PORTFOLIOS AND JOURNALS

Remember, the purpose of assessment is multifold: Teachers want to better understand students through assessment, but the ultimate path to student liberation is for students to use assessment as a means to better know themselves. Assessment should not be used to control learners, encourage competition, or otherwise fortify a system that continues to make students objects of learning. Assessment, instead, should tell a story—and our students should play a significant role in telling that story. While tools like learning objectives and rubrics may run the risk of dehumanizing learning—that is, if they are used improperly—taking a portfolio- and/or journal-based approach to assessment contextualizes these tools within a child's broader learning journey, helping parents and students alike see that rubrics and checklists merely serve as concrete tools that provide a common language and structure in which to reflect on learning. The real assessment, however, happens when students use the tools and the language they provide as scaffolds for identifying strengths, citing challenges, and telling the story of their progress as a learner.

Both journaling and digital portfolios are visual in nature, and by keeping artifacts organized within journals and/or portfolios, students can easily flip back through them to compare work from previous lessons or units. I'll show you a few examples of journals in the next chapter. Ultimately, when journals and portfolios are used well, they become concrete examples of what it looks like when we use assessment *as* learning (Gottlieb, 2016). This is distinct from assessment that informs instruction or standardized assessments that norm or categorize students; this is assessment that speaks in a concrete, visual, and student-friendly language, liberating them from comparing themselves to others or reaching for arbitrary benchmarks. They can, instead, strive to continuously become the best version of themselves.

"Wow!" I said to Annabelle. "Your handwriting looks incredible!"

She looked up and smiled, but it was clear that she wasn't processing just how far she'd come.

"Can I interrupt you for a second? I want to show you how great you're doing."

I sat next to her at our kidney table and flipped back through her journal.

"Look at this! What do you see when you compare these two pages?" I asked.

"Well," she began, "my letters are floating off of the lines and it's kind of hard to read. And now my letters are on the lines, and I can see the spaces between my words."

"I see that, too!" I replied. "How do you think you got there?"

"I'm slowing my hand down more," she replied. "And I think it really helps me to work over here at the kidney table because I'm not as distracted."

"How are you slowing your hand down?" I asked.

"I keep reminding myself that I'll probably have to erase it and do it over if go too fast," she finished.

The truth is that this was a huge accomplishment for Annabelle. It had taken her months to become this self-aware, to articulate this type of self-talk, and to choose a successful spot in the classroom that kept her focused. The beauty of this approach is that it can be applied to virtual distance learning, as well. While students can continue to use their journals at home to reflect on their work in a similar manner, we can also use digital portfolios to help them go back in time and see what their work used to look like. In Seesaw, a digital application for helping students document their work and share it with their parents, students can easily snap pictures of their work and even digitally edit them, marking them up with text or marker. They can even record their voices over their documents, creating yet another easy way to verbally reflect on their work.

Toward the end of our final math unit for the year, all of which took place virtually, I wanted my students to see just how far they'd come in their understanding of geometry and geometrical measurement. They had just taken their final assessments, and I had just gone through them, leaving feedback and asking them to make corrections. After they made their corrections, I had them reflect using our typical strengths and challenges reflection T-chart.

Unit 5 Math Reflection	
Celebrations	**I'm still working on...**
1) I can tell many shapes apart. 2) I used to identify shapes by colors, but now I identify them by attributes more.	1) knowing when it's a rhombus. 2) noticing if the scale is one unit or two units. 3) reviewing my work before submitting it; I made some errors I didn't need to make.

Not only would these artifacts become part of their digital portfolios, allowing them to reflect on their learning even after our time together had concluded, but they were also able to use their portfolios to reflect on earlier assessments from the unit, conveniently stored in Seesaw and allowing them to look back on them with ease.

Once again, this is not a tool that needs to be saved only for distance learning. Using digital portfolios to support reflection is a great way to build independence in students during in-person learning, as well.

REDEFINING STUDENT SUCCESS

When we humanize assessment, we redefine what it means to be successful in our classrooms, and in an age where we are being challenged to rebuild our education system in a more equitable and inclusive manner, redefining student success is where we must begin.

In this chapter, we talked about identifying the purpose behind assessment, as well as identifying standards for learning that support students in their futures as lifelong learners. We also discussed a couple tools for assessment that bring students into the process, empowering them as we partner with them to cultivate self-awareness around their strengths and challenges. You'll notice that none of these tools force students to compare themselves to one another, and that none of these assessment practices rigidly categorize or track students. To do so would operate in opposition to equity and humanized learning. Instead, these tools and practices only ask students to examine themselves in comparison to past versions of themselves—to reflect for the purpose of on-going growth.

Ultimately, when building independence within our students, that is how we want to define success. Students in humanized classrooms are successful when they reflect on their learning and initiate changes to their work or their learning habits on their own. These are the true skills of a lifelong learner, and these are the skills we should be continuously cultivating within our students. Best of all, when we redefine success in our classrooms, we allow our pedagogy to shift, as well, to a practice that centers equity and our students' humanity.

TIPS FOR TEACHING FROM A DISTANCE, CHAPTER 6

- Think of assessment as a partnership between students and teachers. Share some of the power.

- Explain to your students the *why* behind assessment. When they know the purpose, they will be more likely to buy into it.

- Be mindful of *what* you're assessing. Standards and standardized assessments have been weaponized against students for years.

- Remember that *how* you assess matters most. Humanizing assessment means using it as a tool for better knowing and understanding students as human beings.

- Redefine student success in your classroom not as achievement in relation to grade-level standards, but instead as progress measured against students' previous versions of themselves.

CHAPTER SEVEN

LEVERAGING COMPLEX INSTRUCTION

By now, it should be clear that the practices that are giving us trouble during distance learning were practices that were problematic before we were forced to teach virtually. The pandemic, in many ways, is challenging us to change; it's providing us an opportunity to innovate and permanently change our approach to teaching and learning for the better.

Teachers are not to blame for the perpetuation of these flawed practices. Some scholars of educational equity would argue that our education system is doing exactly what was designed to do—to serve the interests of our most privileged and powerful citizens. When we consider that this system is a product of white supremacist and patriarchal thinking, it stands to reason that our pedagogies mirror and place value on such thinking. Think back to the fourteen characteristics of white supremacy culture that appear in the first chapter of this book.

We see *perfectionism* in our students' (and their parents') challenges with taking risks and making mistakes; we see *quantity over quality* in terms of our emphasis on work completion and "point totals"; we see power hoarding when we create learning tracks that only allow a limited number of students (typically those who are white and middle class) to participate in "honors" classes or access higher-level content; we see *individualism* in the latest push for personalized learning practices that have students consuming content that is marketed as "just right" for them, based only on arbitrary quantitative indicators; we see *either/or thinking* in the context of multiple-choice tests that are more likely to measure privilege than they are to capture a child's strengths, challenges, and action steps.

But most of all, we see *paternalism*. When one acts with *paternalism*, they operate with a mindset that those of lesser status are unable to make decisions on their own. In many cases, those who act paternalistically believe they're doing something noble by making said decisions. And while perhaps it is possible that when teaching children, we must make some decisions on their behalf—for instance, in terms of what makes most sense to be learned within developmental ranges—we don't have to do so in a way that promotes hovering over students, robbing them of their autonomy and sense of purpose. We can do so in a way that emboldens them, helps them learn to make their own choices, and encourages them to stand on their own two feet.

WHAT IS COMPLEX INSTRUCTION?

At first glance, the gradual release model (Pearson & Gallagher, 1983) for teaching seems appropriate for fostering student independence. But with further thought and consideration, the *I do, we do, you do* structure has its limits, and if overused, can create a codependency between teachers and students: Teachers can't function without a linear and didactic model for filling students' minds with bits of knowledge or teaching them replicable procedures, and likewise, students can't learn without teachers spoonfeeding them skills, bit by bit and lesson by lesson.

That's not to say that modeling is bad. In fact, sometimes modeling is necessary to help students envision an end goal or end product. That said, an overreliance on modeling puts all the onus on the teacher, with students becoming skilled in the process of copying or replicating skills, as opposed to co-constructing knowledge with their teachers and peers. What's more, when we operate from this model of *I do*, then *we do*, then *you do*, we operate in opposition to equity in our classrooms. The likelihood that even a majority of our students are ready for any one given strategy or tool is small. As a result, we need to diversify the strategies to which we expose our students, allowing them to leverage a toolbox of strategies for productive and independent learning, as opposed to simply modeling algorithms or strategies for regurgitation on a test.

The alternative begins with rethinking our pedagogy and challenging ourselves to teach for independence so that, in some ways, students will always be learning from a distance, equipped with the necessary tools to stand on their own. This could also, perhaps, offer us insight into why distance learning has gone so poorly for so many teachers. During in-person learning, teachers have the luxury of walking around the classroom, re-modeling strategies or giving feedback as students are working. During virtual distance learning, we are no longer afforded this luxury. To a certain degree, students must be self-reliant, and they must have some strategies that allow them to attempt assignments on their own before relying on a teacher to didactically model and re-model skills. Moving away from this linear and didactic model for teaching and learning is a step toward something that is truly human-centered and needs-based.

Learning is part of the human condition. It just isn't natural to dislike learning. Students end up disengaging from learning because they don't connect intrinsically with learning experiences: they either don't understand the purpose behind learning a specific skill or are not afforded the opportunity to make choices while learning. The aforementioned gradual release model reinforces both a lack of purpose and the limiting of choice. By modeling and then simply asking our students to copy what we've modeled, we strip our students of any element of choice and limit their ability to find purpose in what they're doing. After all, what's the purpose in copying something directly, other than compliance? And what's the purpose in taking a risk, making a mistake, or trying something new when there's only one way to complete a task?

Complex instruction provides an alternative to the gradual release model. It offers us an opportunity to make our curriculum open ended and allow for inquiry-based and constructivist experiences that center student agency and independent learning, and only using modeling when students really need it.

Coined in 1997 by researchers Elizabeth Cohen and Rachel Lotan, the term "complex instruction" refers to a philosophy of teaching that meets three criteria:

1. Multiple-ability curricula

2. Special instructional strategies that foster collaborative learning

3. Ensuring equal access to learning by recognizing and treating problems related to status and inequity

In essence, when we teach with complex instruction in mind, we center both equity and our students' humanity.

By teaching with multiple-ability curricula, we create an inclusive curriculum that allows students of varying abilities the opportunity to work with both ability-similar and ability-dissimilar peers. This is especially important for learning tasks that must be delivered virtually, as preserving a sense of community and connectedness is critical in a time of crisis where students are forced to learn from home. That said, multiple-ability curriculum also promotes equity in the classroom. Many educators falsely believe that, in order to differentiate instruction or curriculum for students, they must provide students with different tasks that appeal to various "levels." But this theory for differentiation presumes that some students are strong in a given content area, and that others are weak. It plays into an industrialized model for teaching and learning that rank orders students, ultimately threatening equity in the classroom.

The reality is that our students enter our classrooms at varying levels of readiness, but that doesn't mean we have to plan in a way that exacerbates these discrepancies between students. We should, instead, be showing students the ways in which they can collaborate across their differences and learn from one another through open-ended tasks that offer access points for all different types of learners.

Complex instruction can be easily demonstrated through math, although it can be leveraged in the literacies and the sciences, as well. Take this simple task that I used with my class this past spring during distance learning:

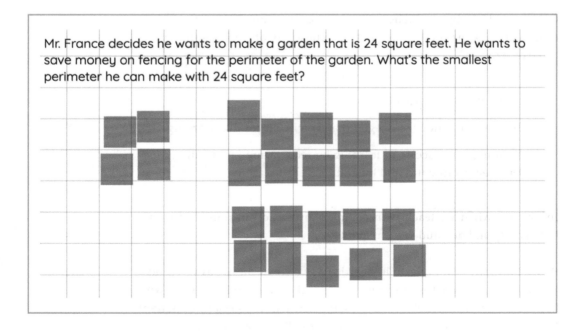

Mr. France decides he wants to make a garden that is 24 square feet. He wants to save money on fencing for the perimeter of the garden. What's the smallest perimeter he can make with 24 square feet?

When designing this task, I kept a couple of things in mind. First and foremost, I embedded it within a *real-world context*. In this case, I was trying to save money on fencing for a garden. Using a real-world context shows students that math is, in fact, important in the real world, meanwhile helping them see the connection between math concepts like area, perimeter, and money. By using *real-world tasks*, we send students the message that understanding math matters and has a purpose in their lives. It can even save you money! Second, I made sure I had *a task that could be solved in multiple ways*. This provided varying access points for a diverse group of students, hence the term "multiple-ability" curriculum, but also allowed us to analyze various methods and discuss their efficiency, cultivating important intellectual skills that foster independence.

While the task itself addressed problems of access and status between my students by allowing for multiple access points, so did the scaffold I put in place. You'll notice an assortment of brown squares scattered about the grid. These squares were intended for students who needed a concrete manipulative to help them navigate the problem. While some students were able to navigate this problem from a representational stage where they simply drew a series of rectangles as plausible solutions, a significant subset of my students required the squares to successfully navigate the problem.

Our class discussion also addressed issues of status and access by allowing students of all levels to share methods. In fact, when planning for these sorts of lessons, I like to plan by anticipating student responses ahead of time. In doing so, I am able to anticipate a discussion where I can "tell a story" of student understanding. The "story" would start with less efficient or less sophisticated methods and gradually grow toward greater efficiency and sophistication.

Figure 7.1 shows what this lesson might look like with the five-question lesson planning structure, with an added component for anticipating responses:

Figure 7.1: Five-Question Lesson Planning Template (Fencing Task)

Question 1: What do I hope students will leave knowing or be able to do?

Students will understand that the perimeter of a rectangle can change even though the area stays the same. Students will also understand that the smallest perimeter for a given area can be found by decreasing the difference between the lengths of the sides.

Question 2: How will I know if students understand this?

I will review students' electronic math journals as they submit them in Seesaw. I will also check in with them in small groups while they're working to gauge problem-solving strategies.

(Continued)

Question 3: What instructional resource will I use to provoke curiosity and discussion?

Math Task: Mr. France decides he wants to make a garden that is 24 square feet. He wants to save money on fencing for the perimeter of the garden. What's the smallest perimeter he can make with 24 square feet?

Students will also have access to digital manipulatives that will ensure access for all learners.

Question 4: How will I facilitate the discussion or minilesson?

I will use a series of anticipated responses to guide the discussion, beginning with responses that demonstrate a concrete stage of mathematical thinking, gradually moving to a more abstract stage of thinking:

Concrete	Representational	Abstract
Student uses brown squares to guess and check by calculating the perimeter by counting or adding the lengths of sides.	Students draw various rectangles and label them, using the formula for calculating perimeter ($P = 2l + 2w$).	Students reason with the different perimeters, demonstrating that the overall perimeter decreases as the difference between the lengths of sides decreases.

During the discussion, I will ask students to ask questions and comment on the methods their peers share, using discussion prompts previously learned in class.

Question 5: How will we reflect on this lesson?

Students will use the following reflection stems to reflect on new learning in their math journals:

- I used to think . . . Now I think . . .
- _____'s method was most efficient because . . .
- Next time, I am going to try _____'s method because . . .
- I am still confused about . . .
- I am still wondering . . .

You'll notice in the unit plan that I refer to a list of discussion prompts that were used previously. These discussion prompts fall into the "special instructional strategies to foster collaborative learning" that I referred to in the initial definition for complex instruction. When students are engaging in complex instruction during in-person learning, dialogue and discourse at their tables is critical. Granting students time to discuss the task with their groups creates points of convergence, but we cannot assume that they will come into our classrooms, whether virtual or in-person, knowing how to do this on their own. We have to explicitly teach them how to talk about their learning. This is where the discussion prompts come in.

Earlier in the year, after observing my colleague and master teacher, Meghan, lead a math discussion in her classroom, I realized my students were lacking a critical skill, and that this was stopping them from having quality discussions on their own. In order for complex instruction to work, students need to be able to ask questions, add thoughts, and push back on their peers' thinking independently. I realized I needed to create a list of discussion prompts with them to scaffold this skill for them (Figure 7.2). Together, we created this list of discussion prompts, in order to support their independence with math discussions:

Figure 7.2: Discussion Prompts

? Questions to Ask:

- How can you prove this?
- Why does this make sense to you?
- Did you have any other solutions?
- What made you choose this method?
- Can you tell me more?
- Are you saying . . .? (Clarifying question)

+ Thoughts to Add:

- How has your thinking changed?
- Here's another way . . .
- This reminds me of . . .
- This connects to my strategy because . . .
- I agree because...
- What would happen if . . .?

▲ Pushback:

- Have you considered?
- Is there anything more efficient?
- I disagree because...
- Next time, what might happen if you . . .?

Once my students had this language and an anchor chart to which they could easily refer, our whole-group math discussions gradually became much more student-driven. I'd even hear them independently using the discussion prompts at their tables while working through tasks.

During virtual distance learning, students can use these discussion prompts at "virtual tables," leveraging the breakout groups function in Zoom or perhaps even creating separate Google Meet calendar invitations for students to access during small-group work. Another one of our projects for the end of the year, research clubs, also entailed a great deal of small-group work. In this case, I used separate calendar invitations, allowing me to pop in and out of their small-group meetings, provide feedback, and check in on collaboration skills.

This is a major paradigm shift, I know. I'll admit that I found a great deal of comfort in the gradual release model, but trust me when I promise that this will not only radically change your teaching for the better, it will also make distance learning easier for you. The choice to engage in complex instruction over didactic or direct instruction, leads to dismantling problematic practices that oftentimes engender dependent learning habits. We move from *perfectionism* to *vulnerability*, from *either/or thinking* to a flexible *tolerance of uncertainty*, and from *paternalistic pedagogy* to *productive and trusting partnerships* with students, ultimately building relationships with students to teach from a healthy distance, granting them ample opportunities to stand on their own and guide their own learning.

MULTIDIMENSIONAL LEARNING

The reason that complex instruction and the workshop model work so well is because they are multidimensional. They allow students to channel their independence in the whole group, in small groups, and through independent work. This can happen because all three dimensions are all connected to one another, despite the fact that they all serve different purposes in a personalized classroom.

Many teachers have become reliant on traditional didactic models for teaching and learning that leverage direct instruction because they appear to be the most efficient. Yet the need for "efficiency" (a term that was popularized at the height of the industrialized age) reflects white supremacist values in that it is typically symptomatic of a palpable *sense of urgency* that all of us have felt at one point or another while teaching. From overreliance on big data (standardized assessments, in particular) to merit-based ideologies that influence teacher evaluation practices, educators are incentivized to operate with this *sense of urgency*, which is often counterproductive to student liberation and free thought. Productive learning requires cognitive dissonance, and embracing cognitive dissonance means slowing down and sitting with the thoughts that have created a dissonance within us. When we intervene too early and relieve cognitive dissonance on our students' behalves, we actually take away opportunities to learn and reinforce a paternalistic pattern of behavior that engenders dependence. Teaching well from a distance necessitates letting go of this sense of urgency. We need to remind ourselves that the best thing for our students is to give them the time and space they need to resolve their dissonance in their own time, and only with supports that are least restrictive to productive and independent learning.

Embracing the workshop model in our classrooms asks us to move away from purely didactic teaching. In case you're unfamiliar, the workshop model consists of three key components: the minilesson, the workshop, and the debrief.

It's true that modeling may be appropriate in some minilessons, though I would argue that these are few and far between. Modeling how to use learning tools like math manipulatives or perhaps even modeling letter formation may be in the best interests of students, but even handwriting is something students need to practice on their own within an authentic context, nullifying the desire to teach in a didactic manner only for regurgitation. Most often, minilessons are best for fostering whole-group discussion around a given topic, modeling flexibility with tools or strategies for learning, or even simply offering suggestions for strategies that students can take or leave, given their needs.

In Writing Workshop, I use a practice called "shared writing" (Routman, 2004) quite a bit. In shared writing, the teacher generally "holds the pen," allowing students to verbally offer ideas while the teacher captures them on the easel or screen. During virtual distance learning this past spring, I still managed to leverage this powerful practice, creating a sense of community while modeling a strategy for revising our fairy tales.

Aimee Buckner's book *Notebook Know-How* (2005) is an excellent resource for building student independence through writing strategies. When teaching writing, especially to young students, we must center student liberation. Being a good writer means being a liberated thinker. Students who write well know how to work through obstacles, think flexibly, and apply strategies that help them draft and revise their ideas after receiving feedback or reflecting on their work. On this day, in particular, I was modeling how to "lift a line," as Buckner calls it in her book. When lifting a line, students identify a single phrase or sentence in their writing and then write as much as they can about it, adding sensory details, dialogue, or other forms of description. I find this to be an excellent tool for building independence in my students with regard to revising. By allowing them to draft freely and then use revising strategies like lifting a line retroactively, they are not bogged down by getting it right the first time, and instead have a flexible strategy for continuously improving their writing.

This is an excellent example of how to use a minilesson to model a flexible strategy and incorporate student voice in the process. The day prior, the students and my co-teacher, Logan, had come up with an idea to write a story called *The Three Pandas Fluff*, a fairy tale adaptation of *The Three Billy Goats Gruff*. The initial draft was strong, as this was our second round of adapting fairy tales, but as I always tell my students, "A writer's work is never done."

"Let's find a line to lift," I said, as I read our work from the day before aloud.

We reached a line in the story that seemed like it could use a bit more description. *The three pandas pranced through the forest*, it said.

"Hmm, I'm wondering how we can help readers make more of a mental movie," I said.

I used an additional tool to aid in word retrieval and first had the students brainstorm a list of words that we could use to describe the setting (Figure 7.3). By unmuting or typing ideas into the chat, my students came up with a list of words.

Figure 7.3: Google Slide of Words to Describe the Setting

```
5.14.2020
        Lift a Line: Setting

Words to describe the setting:          -  damp or humid; warm
   -  tall trees                        -  mud oozing through their
   -  pretty blue sky                      toes; squish
   -  vines and leaves from the
      trees                             Original line: The three
   -  grass and mud                     pandas pranced through the
   -  other animals                     forest
        -  chirping
        -  swishing                           They wandered in
        -  rustling                     and out of tree stumps,
        -  elephants trumpeting         looking up to see the pretty
        -  breeze pushing and           blue sky hiding behind a
           swaying, whistling, like     canopy of green leaves. Their
           a flute                      feet squished in mud, oozing
   -  feel the textures on the          between their toes as they
      leaves                            walked, looking for their
                                        favorite bamboo field.
```

Source: Adapted from Buckner, 2005.

We then took this series of words and used them to describe the chosen line in greater depth. Here's what they came up with, using the list of words:

The three pandas pranced through the forest. They wandered in and out of tree stumps, looking up to see the pretty blue sky hiding behind a canopy of green leaves. Their feet squished in mud, oozing between their toes as they walked, looking for their favorite bamboo field.

The differences between the initial line and the new paragraph, while marked and describable, cannot be easily quantified within a checklist or rubric. They need to be experienced within the collective consciousness of the class and compared only to what was written before, not to an arbitrary indicator of success. It is within examples like these that we see the power and purpose of a minilesson. It builds a collective consciousness, preserves connectedness between students, and also offers valuable opportunities for modeling flexible strategies to be applied during the workshop.

After the minilesson, my students ventured off and began working on their own, allowing me time to check in with students in small groups. Normally, during in-person learning, I would call groups of students to my kidney table or perhaps just circulate and provide students feedback while they were at their desks. In our digital environment, I used Google Hangouts. I kept groups of students on speed dial, circulating through almost every group over the course of a given instructional block. By keeping my minilessons to ten or fifteen minutes at a maximum, I maximized my small-group meetings and individualized conferences, giving me actionable data on how my students were faring and which of my lesson ideas I'd choose from for the next day. In some cases, I discovered that I needed a lesson I hadn't anticipated, allowing me to pivot with less than twenty-four hours' notice, still using my desired results and assessment criteria as a North Star to guide me through the uncertainty of this student-driven way of teaching.

While checking in with small-group and individual students, I noticed that students were in all different places. Some were still drafting and needed to dedicate their time and energy to keeping up the momentum. Others were ready to lift lines and began applying the minilesson directly. Some were editing and revising simultaneously, exercising a level of independence for which others weren't ready. And, of course, I had some students who were struggling to get any writing done.

I spoke with DJ over a private conference, as one of his parents had sent me an e-mail saying that writing was especially challenging for him lately.

"Hey, DJ," I said. "What's up? How are things going?"

"I don't know what to write for my introduction," he said. "I don't know how to start my story."

It was clear that he didn't have too much written and that I needed to unblock him. I also knew, however, that simply doing it for him wasn't going to get him anywhere. I had a sneaky suspicion that this was less a matter of having words to write and more a lack of strategies for getting unblocked.

"You know, DJ," I said with a smirk on my face, "there's a strategy we learned recently for this one. It will help you generate a few ideas that you can choose from."

I paused, trying to honor as much wait time as possible, giving him the space to think on his own.

"Lift a line?" he asked after a long pause.

"Not quite," I replied. "There's another one you could use."

"Oh, Try Ten!" he exclaimed.

"Yes, that's the one," I added reassuringly, referring to another one of Aimee Buckner's strategies, Try Ten, where students either rewrite the same line ten times or brainstorm ten ways to say something. "Let's use Try Ten to come up with a few different ways to open your story. Do you have any ideas for how to start?"

"I could start with 'Once upon a time . . . ' That's how a lot of fairy tales start," DJ proposed.

"That's a great idea," I said. "Write that down and finish the sentence."

He followed suit, and through a discussion with me, he came up with a few more ideas for opening his story. I don't always require students to "try" all ten, especially if trying only three or four alternatives gets them unstuck.

"So which one do you like the most?" I asked.

"I think I like number two the most," he said to me.

"Great! Let's use it, and when we get off the call here, I want you to see if you can write a whole page before the end of writing workshop," I said, making sure to identify a clear and concrete goal with him. "I don't want you to worry about it being perfect. I want you to be flexible and measure your success by how much you've written today. Sound good?"

He replied in the affirmative, and I could tell he was ready to write.

"One more thing," I said to him. "I want to take a moment to reflect. I'm just curious if you noticed what I did today to help you."

"You helped me remember to use Try Ten," he said, in so many words.

"You're exactly right," I replied. "I just reminded you to use a strategy. You did everything else on your own. In fact, I hardly helped at all! What do you think you could do next time on your own to get yourself unstuck?"

"I can try ten!" DJ said, and we finished our conversation.

It is in these moments we can see the power of the workshop model and its function in building student independence. DJ needed this conference with me. He needed to be reminded of his own independence, and he needed me to meet him right where he was, not only providing him with just enough assistance to get him unstuck, but to also center transferable learning habits that would set him up for increased independence in future situations where he encountered obstacles like these.

In the final portion of the workshop model, the entire class comes back to reflect as a group. Some call this a "debrief," allowing students to discuss what went well and what didn't work, but it can also be an opportunity for students to share what they worked on over the course of a given learning block. In reading workshop, this might look like having students share about the books they read, and in writing workshop, this could entail having students read selections of their writing to demonstrate how they applied the minilesson or made progress on their writing for the day. Not only does this reflection time offer a closing moment for students to bond over their work and share of themselves, it also offers one more chance for me to gather valuable assessment data to inform the following day's lesson.

DEINDUSTRIALIZING LEARNING

By leveraging complex instruction and the workshop model, we do so much more than build independence in our students: We also deindustrialize our curriculum and the learning process. It stops us from worrying about completing work or covering content, and instead, challenges us to make every lesson a new chapter in a child's learning narrative.

Take, for instance, worksheets and workbooks. These play into the idea of *quantity over quality*, helping adults, and perhaps even some students, feel better about "how much" they've learned by concretely seeing how much work they've completed. Textbooks, too, are indicative of the industrialization of curriculum. Textbooks package information for students to consume, as opposed to helping students discover new ideas and construct knowledge with their peers.

That's not to say that trade books aren't helpful in the classroom, especially if we ensure they're reflective of a range of voices and identities and written by a diverse group of authors. That's also not to say that the occasional reproducible isn't helpful. Sometimes a graphic organizer or other reproducible is developmentally appropriate and supportive of equity, especially if it offers diverse groups of students opportunities to collaborate through varied entry points. But by and large, I believe learning should be taking place in journals, allowing students to have a hand in documenting what's going on in their minds, as opposed to reproducing spoon-fed knowledge or filling in a series of blank boxes on a worksheet.

In the beginning of the year, I spend far more time modeling how to use our journals than I do challenging students' thinking with new learning experiences and provocations. That said, in most schools I've worked, journaling is not a pervasive practice in every subject, meaning that it's the first time my students have encountered such a journal-centric way of teaching and learning.

I have three types of journals in my classroom: the math journal, the writer's notebook, and the thinking journal, each of which is governed by structures and strategies that foster independence in students.

MATH JOURNALING

I learned about math journaling from Meghan Smith, the master math teacher, who I mentioned earlier in this chapter. She is, hands down, one of the most gifted math teachers I've ever witnessed, and my practice is forever changed from watching her. She introduced me to the journal structure: My Idea, My Thinking, New Learning, Reflection. Using this structure, independent student learning is scaffolded through the clear and reliable structure, meanwhile supported by classroom discussions that expose students to various problem-solving methods. Figure 7.4 is an example using the garden fence problem from earlier, demonstrating how a student might use the virtual task on Seesaw paired with a paper journal.

Figure 7.4a and Figure 7.4b: Math Journal Examples

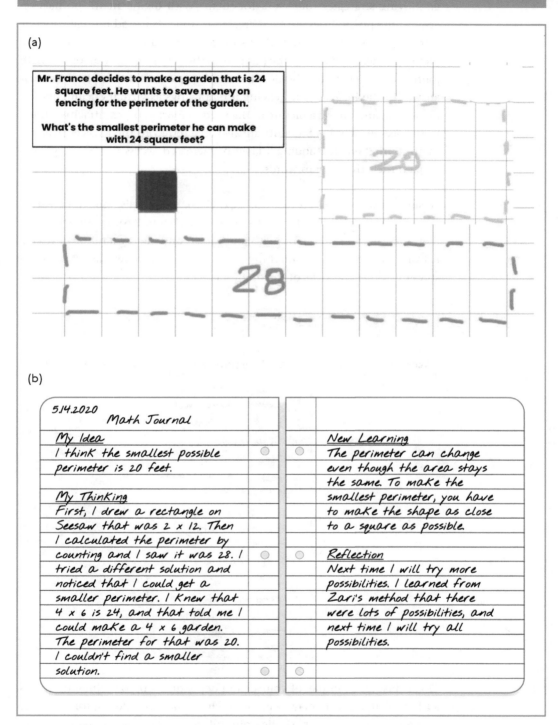

(a)

Mr. France decides to make a garden that is 24 square feet. He wants to save money on fencing for the perimeter of the garden.

What's the smallest perimeter he can make with 24 square feet?

20

28

(b)

5.14.2020
Math Journal

My Idea
I think the smallest possible perimeter is 20 feet.

My Thinking
First, I drew a rectangle on Seesaw that was 2 x 12. Then I calculated the perimeter by counting and I saw it was 28. I tried a different solution and noticed that I could get a smaller perimeter. I knew that 4 x 6 is 24, and that told me I could make a 4 x 6 garden. The perimeter for that was 20. I couldn't find a smaller solution.

New Learning
The perimeter can change even though the area stays the same. To make the smallest perimeter, you have to make the shape as close to a square as possible.

Reflection
Next time I will try more possibilities. I learned from Zari's method that there were lots of possibilities, and next time I will try all possibilities.

As you can see, the math journal allows students to chart their own path, employing strategies that work for them. With digital math journals on Seesaw, the possibilities are even greater. If students use additional concrete learning tools like base-ten blocks or colored counters, they can snap a picture of them and import the photo into the "My Idea" section of the math journal entry. They can also do what this student did and simply write their answer in the idea section, leaving the drawings as virtual documentation on Seesaw, and taking a picture of the written journal pages, attaching them to the Seesaw activity. Students are also able to record their voices over the math journal entries, adding a layer of increased access if they struggle to explain their thinking in words.

To support students in correctly using their math journals, I suggest creating a rubric or checklist to start the school year (Figure 7.5). Doing so clearly identifies success criteria for math journaling, and having a rubric or checklist on hand gives you something to which you can refer back if or when students forget the steps of the math journal.

Figure 7.5: Single-Point Rubric for Math Journaling

Strengths	Math Journaling	Challenges
	☐ I used pictures, numbers, and/or words to share my idea.	
	☐ I explained my steps thoroughly using complete sentences and transition words.	
	☐ I reflected on my learning by sharing a challenge, a success, or how my thinking changed.	
	☐ I used the grids and the lines to organize my thinking as best as I could.	

This is just an example, of course, and depending on your students' needs and challenges, you may want to include different descriptors in your single-point rubric. These single-point rubrics can be made for writer's notebooks and thinking journals, too.

WRITER'S NOTEBOOKS

Writing journals or writer's notebooks can be a bit less structured than math journals, but that doesn't mean they should be without structure. The boundaries we put in place for writer's notebooks should provide productive constraints that help keep things organized, while allowing students to explore themselves and their writing freely.

When I begin the school year, I start by modeling how to use a writer's notebook. I usually make an anchor chart that provides a clear visual example of how it should look, like the example in Figure 7.6.

You can also make a single-point rubric (Figure 7.7) to include on Seesaw or to have them tape into the inside front cover of their writer's notebooks.

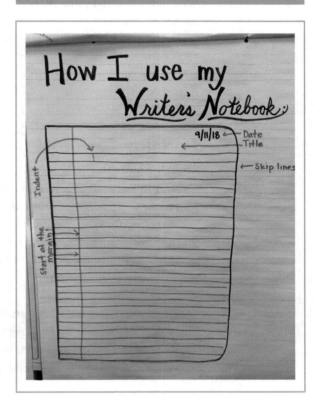

Figure 7.7: Single-Point Rubric for Writer's Notebook

Strengths	Writer's Notebook	Challenges
	☐ I wrote a date and a title for today's entry. ☐ I indented the first word of each paragraph. ☐ My writing hugs the red line (the margin). ☐ I skip lines so that I can go back and revise later.	

It's important to remember that these criteria should be communicated with purpose. Students need to know that dates and titles help them keep track of their work, that indenting for new paragraphs helps readers chunk text in their minds, that using the red line in the notebook maximizes our use of space, and that skipping lines allows us to revise and edit work later without having to squish extra words in between lines. In essence, each of these criteria on the single-point rubric promotes independence in writing workshop, as each of the criteria helps them to use the journaling tool efficiently and effectively, supporting the writing process even when teachers are not sitting next to students.

THINKING JOURNALS

Thinking journals can truly be used for anything. I have my students write about reading, journal about their feelings, and even reflect on social studies lessons in their thinking journals. Depending on the age of your students, you may find that they need varying levels of support in using their thinking journals. For some students, it's easy to sit down and simply write what's inside their minds. For others, it's not. That's why I suggest using a structure similar to the math journal.

For instance, if you are asking students to respond to reading, you can use *My Idea, My Evidence, My Thinking* (Figure 7.8). This simple structure allows students to share what's on their minds, all the while grounding their ideas in evidence from their background knowledge or the text. Here's an example:

Figure 7.8: Thinking Journal Entry (Reading)

9.13.2020
Weslandia

My Idea
I think the lesson in the story is to just be who you are.

My Evidence
In the story, Wesley doesn't really care what the other kids think of him. He just does his own thing creates this whole land of his own. Eventually the kids notice and think it's cool. At the end it says, "he had no shortage of friends."

My Thinking
This reminds me of how I sometimes feel like Wesley does.

I sometimes care too much about what my friends think. I think it's cool how Wesley was just being himself and that he made friends that way.

Students can also use the thinking journal to create Thinking Maps. In the instance shown in Figure 7.9, I had students use Multi-Flow Maps to document what they had learned about the causes and effects of the Chicago Fire.

Figure 7.9: Thinking Journal Entry (Thinking Maps)

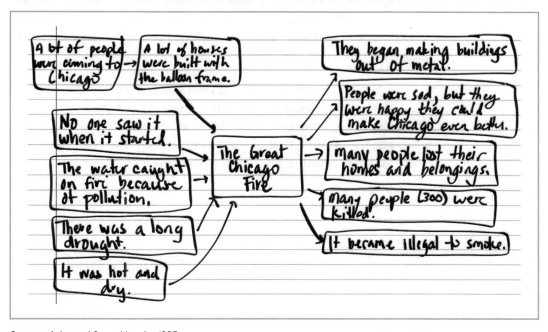

Source: Adapted from Hyerle, 1995.

I've also used the thinking journal to help students process big emotions. As all teachers do, I find that there are moments when I can't stop teaching to help a child process a conflict from recess or resolve their anger. Using the thinking journal as a "feelings journal" can help students contain their feelings and process them independently, allowing them to later share the feelings journal with me when the time is appropriate. For this, I use the structure: *My Feelings, My Story, My Next Steps* (Figure 7.10).

Figure 7.10: Thinking Journal Entry (Feelings Journal)

10.6.2020
Feelings Journal

My Feelings
I am feeling very very angry right now.

My Story
When we were outside at recess, Addison told me she didn't want to be my friend any more. She said it in front of a whole bunch of other kids and they started laughing. I thought it was so mean.

My Next Steps
I want to talk to her about it and tell her how it made me feel.

And finally, I use the thinking journal in social studies, too, leveraging thinking routines to help open students minds and get their thoughts flowing. I maximize my use of images and primary sources in social studies. These allow students to think like historians, using what they notice to make inferences and ask questions. Project Zero has a number of thinking routines that can be easily used in thinking journals (Ritchhart et al., 2011). See-Think-Wonder is only one of the routines that I use to support inferencing and curiosity. Figure 7.11 gives an example from a discussion on income inequality.

The possibilities are truly endless, and what I love most about the thinking journal is that I find new uses for it all the time. That said, the thinking journal should still be governed by productive constraints that support student independence. Figure 7.12 shows an example of a single-point rubric you might use when assessing your students' thinking journals.

Figure 7.11: Thinking Journal (See-Think-Wonder)

2.28.2020

Income Inequality

1970   2017

■ Very High Income ■ High Income □ Middle Income □ Low Income ■ Very Low Income

See:
I see that the dark orange parts of the map spread and that the yellow parts of the map are much less than they were before. I also see that the dark blue got bigger.

Think:
I think this means that some people are getting very rich while others are getting very poor. There's not many middle income people anymore, and I'm thinking maybe this is because laws are unfair.

Wonder:
How did this change? Why are some places able to get richer but others have to get so much poorer?

Map source: Voorhees Center for Neighborhood and Community Improvement.

Strengths	Thinking Journal	Challenges
	☐ I wrote a date and a title for today's entry.	
	☐ I indented the first word of each paragraph.	
	☐ My writing hugs the red line (the margin).	
	☐ I use a structure for the thinking journal if I need it (ie., My Idea, My Evidence, My Thinking)	
	☐ I indented the first word of each paragraph.	
	☐ I elaborate on my thinking by making connections or asking questions.	

But perhaps the best part about journals, in general, is that they free us of the need to print out reproducible after reproducible, and in an era of distance learning where some students may not have access to printers, using journals and the structures that govern them can be a great way to keep kids engaged in academics, meanwhile liberating them by helping them find their voices.

TEACHING FOR LIBERATION

It's sobering to realize that our education system limits independence *by design*—that our education system was never really intended to be democratic or liberating; it was, instead, intended to serve students of privilege, control students and their learning, and enforce passive compliance. When we think of learning blocks as multidimensional, we can begin to promote independence and student liberation. Complex instruction, the workshop model, and flexible learning tools allow students to make their consciousness concrete and their thinking visible. This way, it doesn't actually matter if we're standing right next to them or off to the side while they learn from a distance. They will be independent, empowered, and liberated to learn on their own no matter what.

Imagine, then, how these types of pedagogies will help us dismantle the characteristics of white supremacy embedded within our schools, creating school cultures that instead value:

- Vulnerability
- Presence of Mind
- Openness to Criticism and Feedback
- Quality Over Quantity
- Worship of Independent Thought
- Partnership
- Tolerance of Uncertainty

- Sharing Power
- Sharing Big Feelings and Having Tough Conversations
- Collectivism
- Nonlinear Progress
- Subjectivity and Storytelling
- Embracing Discomfort
- Infinite Ways to Succeed

The truth is we're not that far off from a vision for 21st century teaching and learning that values these ideas. Countless leaders in education, specifically, leaders of color I've referenced through out this book, have already blazed this trail. We may just need to follow them, and the lead the way in our own schools.

Over the course of this book, I've toggled relatively freely between pedagogies for both distance and in-person learning. This is intentional. Quality assessment is quality assessment, from no matter where our students are learning. When I leverage technology for assessment, it is not to streamline multiple-choice assessments into neat spreadsheets; it is a rarity when I do that, if ever. Instead, I use technology during distance learning to ensure that my students may communicate with me just as easily, if not with even greater ease, than they did when we were in person.

The problem with incorporating education technology into our classrooms is that it so frequently increases the complexity of our pedagogy, causing us to mine data from a number of applications, adding to an already overwhelming workload. When leveraging education technology—whether it is for assessment or instructional purposes—it must make our lives easier, not add complexity. It is for this reason that I advocate not for the abandonment of education technology, but instead for an approach to education technology that is minimalist in nature.

TIPS FOR TEACHING FROM A DISTANCE, CHAPTER 7

- Paternalism is a characteristic of white supremacy that is present in mainstream pedagogies. Dismantle this way of operating.

- Use complex instruction to offer open-ended tasks that encourage students to collaborate digitally using video conferencing.

- Leverage the workshop model so that your teaching may be multidimensional, capitalizing on whole-group, small-group, and individualized instruction.

- Deindustrialize your curriculum with journals and use clear structures to support your students when they journal.

- Teach for liberation. Dismantle characteristics of white supremacy and flip them on their heads to codify new values for teaching and learning.

CHAPTER EIGHT

BECOMING AN EDTECH MINIMALIST

To embrace minimalism means to embrace mindfulness and intention. Taking a minimalist approach to education technology doesn't necessarily mean eliminating it altogether; instead, taking a minimalist approach entails being especially mindful when integrating education technology into the classroom, making sure to center equity and humanity at all times.

In the 2020–2021 school year, we had no choice but to increase our dependence on digital technology, and it was with good reason. Resorting to in-person learning inevitably meant putting students, teachers, staff, and families at risk for contracting COVID-19, meaning that in order to keep everyone safe, we had to do distance learning well. In an age of distance learning and beyond—when the nation is back to learning entirely in person—doing distance learning well will mean incorporating technology in a manner that humanizes learning, promotes student independence, and otherwise makes it possible for students to learn no matter where they are.

Perhaps distance learning is also challenging us to permanently change the way that we integrate technology into our classrooms. Our society beckons us to live in excess; we see excess as a sign that we're doing things correctly. There is, however, ample evidence to suggest otherwise. Living in excess is only possible by hoarding wealth and power, inevitably oppressing those with less privilege. Living in excess results in generating a great deal of waste, undoubtedly contributing to the destruction of our little blue planet. And in the classroom, living in excess means our lives become more complicated, stressful, and challenging.

As a result, becoming an EdTech minimalist entails creating a sustainable approach to integrating technology. This approach does not cause teachers and students to live in excess; instead, this approach incorporates EdTech tools that solve problems without creating new ones. It beckons us to move away from learning that centers tech tools and apps and move toward a pedagogy that centers humanity.

MOVING AWAY FROM APP-CENTRIC LEARNING

It's a common misconception that effective technology integration requires downloading a bunch of applications. This misconception can be attributed in part to the way that we departmentalize and silo content in schools. Teachers commonly believe they need various apps for differing subjects or units, when in reality, this is neither efficient nor effective when integrating education technology. We also feel this tendency to download application after application because education technology companies are exceptionally good at selling us technology. Of course, it's not bad to pay for a resource or tool if it truly will make your classroom— be it virtual or in person—a more humanized and sustainable place to teach and learn, but we also must remember that the primary motivation of a technology company is to turn a profit. If they don't turn a profit, they cease to exist.

The 2012–2013 school year was my first experience teaching in a 1:1 environment, meaning one device to one student. My team of fourth- and fifth-grade teachers and I made a conscious choice to move away from an app-centric pedagogy that required countless apps. Our colleague, Katy Fatalleh, had piloted 1:1 devices the year prior, and when it was expanded to our whole team, we were able to leverage the wealth of knowledge that Katy's experience brought us.

Instead, we leveraged a limited number of tools on the iPad that supported students' abilities to make their thinking visible, make the abstract concrete, or otherwise make the documentation of learning more streamlined and sustainable. Looking back, I'll admit that even with this philosophy that limited our dependence on applications, I was still overusing the iPads. Not only did I limit my use of paper notebooks and do primarily word-processing tasks, I also began flipping my classroom.

In case you're unfamiliar, flipping the classroom is a technology-driven practice where teachers post instructional videos, require that students view the videos for homework, and then take an assessment upon entering the classroom. The results of this assessment are then used to group students and provide activities that meet them at their current level of proficiency. At the time, this was a cutting-edge practice, but in hindsight, I now know that this manner of flipping the classroom was operating in opposition to educational equity. It also created an unsustainable workload for me, as every math class required me to do the following:

1. Plan three or four sets of activities for students of differing "levels" during the in-person portion of the class

2. Create an instructional video for homework

3. Write an accompanying formative assessment for completion upon entry to class

While flipping the classroom created the perception that I was differentiating my instruction, it also resulted in tracking my students. The students who struggled with the entry assessment were usually the same handful of students, and likewise, the students who met expectations or excelled were usually the same groups of kids. Ultimately, tracking operates in opposition to educational equity, as it widens instructional gaps between students.

This type of model for learning also centered content consumption; it didn't center problem-solving or student independence. The daily instructional videos I created and posted to my classroom website were reminiscent of the gradual release model, where I simply modeled *how* to do something, removing dialogue and discourse from the learning process. In fact, I'd go so far to say that it wasn't really *learning*, per se; it was a compliance model that institutionalized mathematics and my students.

Flipping the classroom is an excellent example of what happens when we operate without minimalism in mind. I was convinced that *more was more*, and that maximizing my use of digital technology would help me make the most of my time. But in actuality, this approach chipped away at student independence, disembodying my classroom community by tracking students, and creating a curriculum that prioritized content consumption. Integrating technology in a student-centered manner requires a different approach. It requires making the most of screen time by maximizing active screen time; it necessitates minimizing quantitative data by leveraging digital technology to expand opportunities for qualitative assessment; and most of all, it requires integrating technology in a manner that either preserves or enhances human connection.

MAXIMIZING ACTIVE SCREEN TIME

There are a lot of opinions out there about screen time, and I agree that limiting screen time is important, especially for our youngest learners. The research is clear that too much screen time can have adverse effects, including but not limited to negative effects on sleep (American Academy of Pediatrics, 2016). But in 2020, we were left with few good choices. Did we concentrate large groups of students in small spaces, forcing them to sit in their desks all day to learn in person? Or did we keep them home, limiting in-person socialization and increasing screen time?

The truth is that all types of screen time are not created equal, and that if we use screen time in a way that is sustainable and student centered, we can minimize its adverse effects. Active screen time—screen time that centers problem-solving, cognition, or human interaction—is much different than passive screen time—which is screen time that requires little to no thought, interaction, or mindfulness (Sweetser et al., 2012). When requiring screen time for learning, either during in-person learning or while engaging in distance learning, we should be maximizing our students' active screen time, ensuring that when interacting with screens, they are doing so in a way that promotes active thinking and mindfulness as opposed to sedentary activity.

There is not a fine line between active and passive screen time. Instead, it operates on a spectrum, and as teachers, we must exercise restraint in labeling a given activity as "active" screen time simply because it requires a student to answer questions or process information. I would argue that the aforementioned practice of flipping the classroom leans toward passive screen time, despite the fact that my approach to flipping required students to complete a workbook page while watching my instructional videos. In comparison to what I advocate for in Chapter 7, the practice was quite mindless because I wasn't asking my students to think nearly as much as I do when using complex instruction, teaching through problem-solving, and engaging my students in dialogue and discourse. At its best, my "flipped" videos asked students to complete a few problems independently, in an effort to see if they could replicate the method or algorithm I chose to teach. At its worst, students were simply copying answers from the video. When I look back, it may have temporarily inflated test scores in my classroom, but it didn't do much in the way of fostering student independence, critical thinking, or problem-solving. Instead, it provided privileges to the students who were capable of quickly acquiring new information and reproducing it the following morning on my entry assessments.

To aid you in identifying active screen time, Figure 8.1 provides a single-point rubric for you to self-assess your practice. While this can be completed independently, we know that the best learning happens in a group, when learners can engage in discourse about nuanced topics such as active screen time. I would suggest finding a trusted group of teachers—perhaps your grade-level team or department—with whom you can discuss your self-evaluation. I would also suggest citing specific examples of applications or practices that meet the criteria. I've listed some examples after Figure 8.1.

Figure 8.1: Active Screen Time Single-Point Rubric

Strengths	Active Screen Time	Challenges
	☐ Screen time requires students exercise independence in the form of critical thought or problem-solving.	
	☐ Screen time serves a clear purpose within the learning plan, removing barriers or adding value to the student experience.	
	☐ Screen time encourages students to strike a balance between content consumption and creation.	
	☐ Screen time centers human connection in the form of collaboration or interpersonal communication.	

These points are not orthogonal, meaning that they are all interrelated to one another and cannot be neatly divided into separate categories. As a result, examples of what this looks like in practice do not neatly correspond to each point on the rubric. Take, for instance, interactive applications like iCardSort or Popplet, which we briefly discussed in Chapter 5. iCardSort allows students to group digital cards that contain words, ideas, or pictures into categories, reinforcing classification, a valuable cognitive skill essential for problem-solving. Popplet, a child-friendly mind-mapping tool, allows students to make concept maps. Both of these tools require students to *exercise their independence and critical thought*, meanwhile encouraging them to be *strike a balance between creation and consumption*. Sorting words in iCard-Sort or creating a mind map inevitably require some content consumption, depending on the topic you're studying, but these applications also offer students the opportunity to create an artifact that reflects their learning. Simpler tools like Book Creator provide this, too, allowing students to create their own books, perhaps in conjunction with projects in writing workshop, adding extra excitement and creativity into the curriculum.

Additionally, none of these tools—Popplet, iCardSort, and Book Creator—are subject dependent. Instead, they are tools that help students make their thinking and their learning tangible, visible, and concrete, allowing them to use the applications as tools for showing what they know, no matter what they're studying.

Electronic math manipulatives are another great example of both active screen time and mindful technology integration. These manipulatives add productive scaffolds that help all students access classroom content, ultimately *serving a clear purpose in the learning plan* and *removing barriers for students*. Electronic math manipulatives also promote critical thought and problem-solving, as they allow students to concretely show how they've reached an answer when solving a math problem.

MINIMIZING QUANTITATIVE DATA

In the next chapter, we will discuss the detriments of using web-based, adaptive tools for either distance or in-person learning. When I say web-based, adaptive tools, I'm specifically referring to tools that determine students' levels based on an algorithm and then send them content based on their respective levels. By and large, these tools are designed for efficient content consumption, as opposed to creative problem-solving or critical thinking. Teaching through problem-solving or for critical thinking is often messy, inefficient, and unpredictable. Web-based, adaptive tools also provide an immense amount of quantitative data. Not all quantitative data are bad, but an overemphasis on them skews the way our minds think about learning.

The overemphasis on quantitative data is pervasive and equally indicative of white supremacist thinking. Throughout the No Child Left Behind era, policymakers attempted to apply business models to solving all too human problems in the interest of "school reform." Recall that the characteristics of white supremacy (Jones & Okun, 2001) include an emphasis on *quantity over quality*, and this also includes an emphasis on the quantitative over the qualitative. We seek to measure that which was never really meant to be measured with a number, and this way of thinking has significantly impacted the way that technology has been designed for our classrooms. When I was working for the personalized learning company that I mentioned in Chapter 4, I remember one of the engineers asking me if we should build a tool that graded assignments for teachers, in an effort to make our jobs more efficient and sustainable, but inevitably resulting in all assignments being rated with a quantitative indicator.

I replied with an almost immediate and emphatic no. Not only did I know that the qualitative information was far more valuable than the quantitative result of an assessment, I knew that it wasn't necessarily the results of an assessment that helped me understand what my students knew or where they needed assistance. It was, instead, the *process* of assessing student work that helped me analyze their misconceptions and determine what lay at the root of their challenges. I knew that I had to be the one doing the assessing if I wanted to figure out how to best reach my students. Allowing a program to assess on my behalf would have made the process of assessment mindless, product driven, and purely quantitative. Oftentimes, the data that web-based adaptive programs provide create a binary: They've either answered the question correctly or they haven't. Rarely do they provide insight into how the child struggled with the question, or which misconceptions were activated by the problem. They simply tell me if students answered correctly. This is not only a passive way for students to learn from a screen—it's also a very passive way for teachers to teach and assess, reactive in nature and responsive to deficits rather than strengths.

On the contrary, digital portfolios make for active screen time, aiding students in their independence not only by allowing them to document their own work and use assessment *as* learning (Gottlieb, 2016), but also by offering a variety of tools for demonstration of learning. Using a tool like Seesaw, students can take photos of their work, record voice-overs, or even record entire videos to demonstrate areas where they're succeeding and others where they're struggling. There are a number of systems that do this now, and it's simply a matter of finding one that's affordable and user friendly for your class. Something as simple as Google Drive could even be a viable option if organized well.

Portfolio-based assessment provides a way to maximize qualitative assessment. When we assess qualitatively, we are not worried about the number of questions answered correctly; instead, we use student work as a means for determining if students have mastered key skills, using their work samples as evidence for mastery. When using portfolios and centering qualitative assessment, we are able to partner with students to tell the story of their learning journey, using their work samples to describe nuances in their progress that cannot be captured quantitatively, similar to the learning reflections, checklists, or single-point rubrics I shared in the last chapter. These assessment tools do not incentivize students to answer an arbitrary number of questions correctly; they encourage them to describe their learning qualitatively and allow teachers to do so, as well, improving the ways in which we articulate feedback and ultimately help students grow.

CENTERING HUMAN CONNECTION

The year 2020 has taught us that human connection matters most in our classrooms, and I hope this realization motivates all of us to permanently change our pedagogy for the better. In my first book, *Reclaiming Personalized Learning*, I pose four questions to ask yourself before integrating technology:

1. Does the tool minimize complexity?

2. Does the tool maximize individual power and potential?

3. Does the tool reimagine learning?

4. Does the tool preserve or enhance human connection?

All of these questions are important to ask oneself when becoming an EdTech minimalist. We want to be sure we are preserving our energy, only using tools that minimize the complexity of humanizing learning, meanwhile maximizing our potential as individuals in the classroom. However, we shouldn't do so at the expense of poor pedagogy. We have to be sure that we are constantly reimagining learning by taking a human-centered and needs-based approach. The fact is that there is nothing revolutionary about turning on a program and asking students to answer questions in isolation, as many web-based adaptive tools would beckon us to do. We are reimagining nothing when we continue to industrialize learning, albeit through digital means. Above all else, we must be sure that digital technology is giving our students much needed time for socialization, partially in an effort to center their humanity and the intrinsic need to connect with others, but also because we know that by centering human connection, we teach in a way that's natural for students. Learning should always be a conversation, a healthy exchange between human beings. After all, to learn is to be human, and it can't happen in isolation.

Perhaps the most obvious examples of tools that center *human connection* are video conferencing tools like Zoom and Google Meet. These tools can be used flexibly to allow for whole-group instruction in the form of short minilessons, small groups using Zoom Breakout Groups or group calls on Google Hangouts, or even individual conferences where students and teachers can share screens and reflect on work together. Google Docs and Google Slides also support human connection because they allow students to collaborate virtually and asynchronously, when appropriate. Google Docs also allows for the free flow of feedback, with students able to write collaboratively or even share their documents with one another, adding in digital comments or revisions. With these tools, students can offer both validation and critical feedback, allowing the process of assessment to, yet again, be seen *as* a learning tool (Gottlieb, 2016). By teaching students how to give feedback, receive constructive criticism, and otherwise collaborate with peers to make improvements to their work, we are building another set of ancillary skills that are necessary to becoming a lifelong learner.

A NEED FOR ONE ANOTHER

All the tools I've mentioned, as well as the success criteria I've outlined in Figure 8.1, have one thing in common: They center student independence and student liberation. These tools or pedagogies do not engender mindlessness in the learning process or a dependence on education technology that delivers academic content; instead, they encourage students to create and manipulate, demonstrating what they know and are able to do in a manner that works for them.

In his book, *The Empathic Civilization*, Jeremy Rifkin (2010) described technology as a means for empathic extension. Historically, the greatest advancements in technology have helped people come together. They have made the world a smaller place, making it possible for human beings to connect and communicate in ways they never had before and see things in one another that were previously invisible. Technological advancements such as web-based, adaptive tools or other digital solutions that prioritize content consumption do not bring people together; they don't make it easier or more possible for humans to connect over long distances. Instead, they separate them and place them in silos. We can't afford any more social isolation; we can't afford to silo our students any longer.

The COVID-19 crisis has taught us that our students need each other—that connecting is possible even if it has to be done from a distance. The inherently human component of teaching and learning is what our students are craving the most right now, and it's undoubtedly part of the reason why so many pushed to go back to school prematurely. It's why so many couldn't resist heading to bars, restaurants, and other outings, despite the fact that it was not safe. It's clear, more than ever, that we need to be connecting with one another, not mindlessly consuming content on a tablet. We must remember that when choosing classroom technology now and when integrating education technology in person.

TIPS FOR TEACHING FROM A DISTANCE, CHAPTER 8

- Move away from app-centric learning.

- Exercise caution when flipping the classroom, as it may result in an emphasis on content consumption.

- Maximize active screen time and minimize passive screen time.

- Leverage digital technology to provide you new ways to collect qualitative data.

- Be sure your choices in technology are preserving or enhancing human connection.

CHAPTER NINE

DISMANTLING STRUCTURAL INEQUITIES

Divides between students in America became all the more pronounced in 2020. While some schools were able to provide students with the necessary tools to learn from home, others were unable to do so. According to a 2020 report from Common Sense media (Chandra et al.) titled "Closing the K–12 Digital Divide in the Age of Distance Learning," about 30 percent of the nation's students lacked either adequate internet connection or devices to effectively sustain learning at home. Of these 15 to 16 million students who made up almost a third of all students nationwide, over half lacked both.

In some states, approximately half of students lacked digital access, but even in states where fewer students were affected, the numbers were still staggering, with approximately one-quarter of the population struggling to access either adequate internet connection or mobile devices for distance learning. This expands to teachers, as well, with nearly 400,000 educators struggling to teach remotely due to a lack of access to the proper tools.

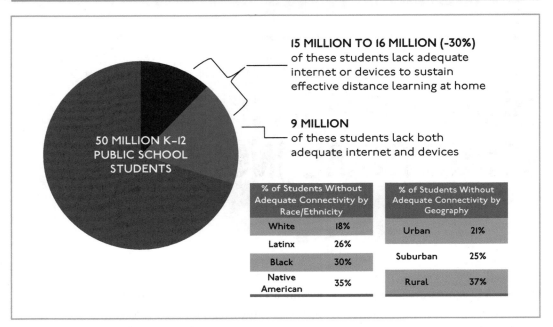

15 MILLION TO 16 MILLION (~30%) of these students lack adequate internet or devices to sustain effective distance learning at home

9 MILLION of these students lack both adequate internet and devices

50 MILLION K–12 PUBLIC SCHOOL STUDENTS

% of Students Without Adequate Connectivity by Race/Ethnicity	
White	18%
Latinx	26%
Black	30%
Native American	35%

% of Students Without Adequate Connectivity by Geography	
Urban	21%
Suburban	25%
Rural	37%

Source: Created using data from Chandra, S., Chang, A., Day, L., Fazlullah, A., Liu, J., McBride, L., Mudalige, T., Weiss, D. (2020).

Students of Color are disproportionately impacted by what we call the Digital Divide (see Figure 9.1). Eighteen percent of white students experience challenges with access to digital technology, while Black and Native American students remain disproportionately affected at 30 percent and 35 percent, respectively. According to the National Center for Education Statistics (NCES, 2020), 2017 data show that Black and Native American students make up 15 percent and 1 percent of students enrolled in primary and secondary schools, respectively. Latinx students made up 27 percent of the school-age population in 2017 and are the only group that is close to proportionately represented in this data, with 26 percent of Latinx students struggling to access digital technology for remote learning. It's important to note that Asian and Pacific Islander students make up approximately 10 percent of the school-age population, according to NCES, and are not represented in the Common Sense Media report (Chandra et al., 2020).

Countless articles have highlighted the self-evident fact that communities of color have been disproportionately affected by the coronavirus pandemic from a health standpoint alone. According to the Centers for Disease Control and Prevention (CDC; 2020), over 20 percent of the people who died from COVID-19 have been Black, despite the fact that only 13.4 percent of the U.S. population is Black. In stark contrast, white people make up about 60 percent of the American population, but only account for about

50 percent of COVID-19 deaths. Considering these data, it becomes abundantly clear that Black people are more at risk than white people (CDC, 2020; U.S. Census Bureau, 2019). This is not due to any biological differences between Black and white people but is instead due to systemic inequities including disproportionate access to quality health care.

Additionally, a September 2020 report from the California Alliance of Researchers for Equity in Education (CARE-ED) noted that households earning greater than $100,000 per year almost universally had access to quality internet, while households that earned less than $30,000 were 60 percent less likely to have access to broadband internet, creating a Digital Divide across socioeconomic demographics, as well.

The COVID-19 pandemic didn't create these inequities; it simply made them more visible than they were before. Such inequities, reflected in ever-widening gaps between rich and poor, institutionalized racism, sexism, homophobia, transphobia, and xenophobia, are longstanding fixtures of American society.

We would be remiss in ignoring the fact that a number of our nation's wealthiest individuals actually managed to *increase* their net worth by billions of dollars over the course of the first six months of the COVID-19 pandemic (Woods, 2020), while conversely, tens of millions of Americans lost their jobs and struggled to simply put food on the table and pay housing expenses. These are red flags—hallmarks of a system that was set up for some to succeed and others to fail. The Digital Divide has been firmly entrenched in the United States for more than thirty years and some estimate that a $12 billion investment could close it (Chandra et al., 2020). While this may seem like a large sum, consider that it is only about one-fourth of Amazon CEO Jeff Bezos's increase in net worth over the course of the COVID-19 pandemic. Perhaps he'd be willing to step in?

Unfortunately, neither Jeff Bezos nor the Trump administration were willing to step in and foot the bill at the start of the 2020–2021 school year. Instead, state and local governments were responsible for sorting out the policies and finances, and teachers were tasked with the tall orders of returning to in-person learning or teaching remotely. Teachers who returned to school in person were asked to do so without the proper protective equipment, adequate ventilation, or room to socially distance. Teachers who were asked to teach remotely were, by and large, provided little training on how to adapt their teaching for a virtual classroom. Some were asked to teach in a hybrid model, serving both students at home and in person. No matter what teachers did, they were asked to make it happen quickly—and with smiles on their faces.

"But let's be clear," Michelle Obama said in her now historic speech at the Democratic National Convention in August of 2020 (WATCH!), "Going high doesn't mean putting on a smile and saying nice things when confronted by viciousness and cruelty. Going high means taking the harder path. It means scraping and clawing our way to that mountain top."

The fact is that this was no smiling matter. For countless educators, it wasn't simply a lack of good choices that made this situation unjust; it was that they had no voice in such decisions. Many schools refused to offer teachers the choice of returning to school in person or teaching from home. Numerous administrators made unilateral decisions on behalf of educators, forcing many of them to decide whether they'd risk their lives in returning to the classroom, temporarily leave the classroom, or perhaps leave the teaching profession altogether. Keep in mind that more than one-quarter of public school teachers are age fifty and over, placing into a higher-risk category for complications from COVID-19. When teachers pushed back, they were faced with gaslighting and toxic positivity. Administrators, parents, and even other teachers tried to convince educators they'd be unaffected by the virus or that their fears were unwarranted. Many who resisted were vilified or told that they could do anything they set their minds to, that they could "do hard things"—even teach in person and subject themselves to a deadly virus in a global pandemic.

Like many who resisted, I was not buying the gaslighting or the toxically optimistic propaganda. Yes, I can "do hard things," but putting myself, my colleagues, and students in harm's way was not a "hard thing." It was an unsafe, unreasonable, and irresponsible request for administrators and politicians to ask this of educators—especially when doing so without their express consent. And no amount of propaganda on social media, telling me that it was my "civic duty" to go back to school and help save the country would have convinced me otherwise.

With that said, a number of the arguments for returning to in-person learning in the fall were compelling, despite the fact that they were weaponized and used as propaganda in an attempt to force teachers into compliance. Some cited food insecurity as a reason for making sure kids were in school, while others noted that child abuse and domestic violence rates were on the rise as a result of quarantining. Others proclaimed that parents would have no options for childcare if schools remained virtual, subjecting parents to even more months of having to balance their employment and their child's school schedule—an undue burden, most certainly, but one that I would hope parents would gladly do if it meant saving lives.

While these arguments are valid and compelling, they beg the question of why, in the richest country in the history of the world, we cannot pass legislation that would address these systemic failings. We have the resources to address food insecurity, but, instead, our regressive tax policies funnel money into the pockets of the richest 1% of individuals in our country. Our government has the power to pass legislation that guarantees childcare to all families (even if only in a crisis) offering stipends to families caring for children, much like we provide caregivers to adults with disabilities.

Throughout the history of school reform in the United States, teachers have been blamed for such systemic failures. We are the people who are blamed, when in reality, we don't have the power to right the compounding wrongs of a system that never really valued us (and many of the students we serve) in the first place.

The "bad teacher" rhetoric reached its height during the No Child Left Behind era, the pinnacle of fear-based, market-based school reform (Kumashiro, 2012). In reality, the vast majority of our teachers are lifelong learners with a sincere desire to continually refine their craft across their professional life cycles. But such rhetoric is the product of a system that has no vested interest in student liberation and free thought, especially if that means empowering Black, Brown, and LGBTQ+ students. Why? Because if the system did that, it would be like setting off an earthquake far beneath the ocean, only to knowingly let it turn into an unstoppable tsunami years down the road. Should our students be truly liberated by a "democratic" and socially just education, it would draw awareness to the oppression and dehumanization of so many in our country, causing an uprising so fierce that the education system, in its current form, wouldn't stand a chance.

"The paradox of education is precisely this," James Baldwin (1963) says, "that as one begins to become conscious, one begins to examine the society in which [they are] being educated."

The education system, in its current form, rests upon the hope that the teachers and learners who occupy the system will not question or critically examine it. Because when we examine the education system in conjunction with the society that contextualizes it, we see that the education system is but a structure that allows long-standing inequities to persist and oppress.

In fact, if we examine the education system closely, we see that it is a mere microcosm for free-market capitalism, situated within a white supremacist society. Ibram X. Kendi, author of *How to Be an Anti-Racist* (2019), refers to capitalism and racism as "conjoined twins," inseparable from one another. In the United States and other industrialized and Westernized nations, the economic success white people have experienced with capitalism begins with the oppression of People of Color, including Native Americans and Black people who were enslaved. Within this system, white people built and continue to maintain structures that funnel wealth, power, and privilege to other white people. They created laws that have kept Black Americans oppressed, from Black enslavement to Jim Crow, and even to school desegregation, a moment in history that has been whitewashed and glorified as a beacon for equity. In reality, the *Brown v. Board of Education* decision served as a mechanism for assimilating Black students into a white education system, operating from a deficit-based mindset that Black schools were defunct and white schools were superior (Gladwell, 2017).

White supremacist and free-market structures continue to inform our education system. They're present in the way we norm standardized assessments and rank-order students from "brightest to dimmest," making it so that, no matter how high students score, there will inevitably be a 99th percentile ranking and a 1st percentile ranking. They're present in the way that we teach students, making them passive receptacles of content and filling their minds with the false narrative that, no matter how hard they work, they can be anything they want. And they're present in the way that our schools are funded, granting schools in predominantly white zip codes with higher home values opportunity to access a greater wealth of resources that inevitably helps students and their families amass even more wealth and privilege as they grow older. These pieces of the puzzle are all connected to one another, and together, they are all responsible for the Digital Divide we currently see in our schools.

A HISTORY OF INEQUITABLE FUNDING

Oak Park, Illinois, a suburb of Chicago, and Lawndale, Illinois, a neighborhood within the City of Chicago, are a mere five miles apart, easily accessible to one another by the Eisenhower Expressway. While they exist only miles apart, they tell quite different stories.

The Oak Park-River Forest (OPRF) school district, serving the towns of both Oak Park and River Forest, boasted an operating budget of $24,863 per student in 2019, while Chicago Public Schools, and by proxy, Lawndale's schools, spent about two-thirds of that at $15,878 per student in 2019, according to the State of Illinois School Report Card (ISRC; 2019a, c).

Bear in mind that Chicago Public Schools were home to a disproportionate number of Students of Color as of 2019, with only 10 percent of the students being white. Oak Park-River Forest, on the other hand, was 55 percent white, with 20 percent Black students, about 12 percent Latinx, nearly 10 percent biracial, 3.5 percent Asian, and 0.1 percent Native American (Illinois State Report Card [ISRC], 2019b, d). While these demographics matter and add context to why these areas are so differently funded, they don't tell the whole story on their own.

In order to understand systems, we must retrace our steps. We must go back in time and ask ourselves how things got this way. By doing so, we reveal clues not only about how systems have evolved into their current form, but also how we can dismantle those systems for a better and more inclusive future.

Like many major metropolitan areas, Chicago and its suburban counterparts are notoriously segregated—and they are because of a series of conscious choices and intentionally racist policies enacted by white people. In his landmark 2014 article, *The Case for Reparations*, Ta-Nehisi Coates writes about Chicago's history of racist housing policies in *The Atlantic*, specifically referring to redlining policies that disenfranchised Black Chicagoans and People of Color, the effects of these policies compounding and echoing into the present day.

He shares the story of Clyde Ross, now long-time resident of Lawndale and a victim of the oppressive housing policies of the 1960s. Ross bought his home "on contract," which meant he wouldn't retain the deed to his home until he paid his loan in full. If, for some reason, he missed one of his unjust and astronomically high payments, his entire home would be taken from him, causing him to lose all of the money he'd paid to the seller up until that point. This was a ploy used by some in those days when selling real estate to Black buyers, allowing them to sell a home multiple times over to different buyers at inflated prices, collecting profits on homes without ever turning over the actual deed. These unfair mortgages and ruthless rules set Black people up to fail, and some white sellers took advantage of that.

Concurrently, the Federal Housing Administration's (FHA) redlining policies peddled racist logic, using color-coding to label some areas as more or less desirable than others. One of the indicators used when determining the desirability of a neighborhood was the presence of "foreigners," as Coates states in his article. The most desirable areas were colored in blue and green, while declining neighborhoods, usually correlating with the number of People of Color moving in, were coded in yellow. When neighborhoods were "redlined," meaning they were color-coded in red, they were labeled as "hazardous" areas, making it nearly impossible to acquire an insured mortgage, and also negatively impacting home values for decades to come.

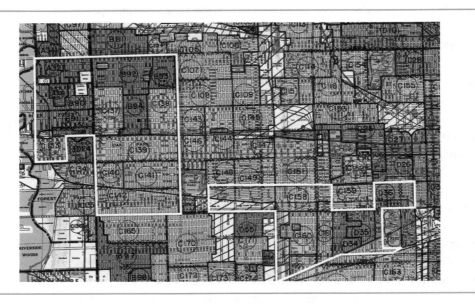

Source: Home Owners' Loan Corporation (1939). "Residential Security Map."

It will likely come as no surprise to you, then, that the OPRF area was barely redlined. In Figure 9.2, the Chicago Redlining Map, we see a mixture of mostly blue, green, and yellow in the OPRF area, suggesting that Oak Park and River Forest were labeled as desirable places to live, no doubt making them destinations for white people who fled cities in the 1950s and 1960s. Despite the fact that today Oak Park and River Forest are seen as relatively diverse and inclusive suburbs, their journey to more equitable housing practices was not a smooth one (Johnson, 2018). In order for homes to be shown to People of Color, residents had to list their homes with an "M" next to them, signaling they could be shown to "minorities." The town also passed an ordinance in 1968, banning the use of for sale signs in front yards. The hope was that this legislation might deter white people from fleeing the area, as a reduction in for-sale signs might make it less obvious how many homes were being sold. It's no small coincidence that parts of the OPRF area were outlined in yellow, signaling a "decline" on the redlining maps, as the area was diversifying and more People of Color were moving in.

Housing prices play a significant role in the funding of our schools, both directly and indirectly, and they've contributed to the modern-day predicament known as the Digital Divide. Local governments account for approximately 45 percent of school funding, with about 80 percent of the local funding coming from property taxes (Reschovsky, 2017). Property taxes are calculated based on a variety of factors, current home values included.

While a home can rise or fall in value based on size or amenities, it can also rise and fall based on the subjective desirability of the neighborhood. A neighborhood's desirability is based off of demand. If a large number of people want to live in a certain neighborhood, the values of those homes will rise. If people decide they don't want to live in a neighborhood for any given reason, the values of those homes will decrease, ultimately decreasing the amount of property tax collected and in effect, decreasing the amount of funding afforded to public schools that serve those particular "undesirable" zip codes.

But the reverse is true, as well. When demand is high and home values rise, schools have an opportunity for even greater funding, as higher home values garner higher property taxes and increased funding. Schools in high-income neighborhoods also benefit from additional endowments or referenda that further fund schools, made possible with disposable income that affluent communities are more likely to have. But the inequity doesn't stop there. Not only are schools in affluent communities already afforded greater funding, the very metrics we use to evaluate our schools have the potential to increase home values as well. Schools that score higher on state report cards are labeled as "high-achieving," inevitably making a neighborhood all the more "desirable." The reality is that these standardized assessments are more likely to measure whiteness and socioeconomic privilege than they are to actually serve as a reliable indicator for a school's effectiveness. As a result, the relationship between home values, test scores, and school funding create a vicious cycle of privilege that continues to afford unearned advantages to those who are able to gain access to the communities where this privilege lies.

In a society like this, where we leverage indicators that measure socioeconomic privilege and whiteness to build structures that reinforce or grow that privilege, we create a perfect storm for compounding educational inequity in our country, one that can only be remedied by large-scale, legislative change to how our schools are funded.

A SYSTEM OF COMPOUNDING INEQUITY

By exploring the history of unfair housing practices and its intersection with how schools are funded in present day, it becomes exceedingly clear from where the Digital Divide originated and how it is an extension of historical systemic inequity. It is neither coincidental nor surprising that Students of Color have been disproportionately impacted by the pronounced educational inequities of the pandemic, considering that their schools were set up to fail prior to the pandemic. We live in a racist system that has created racist policies. These racist policies have built racist structures that are difficult to dismantle. These structures have multiplied their impact, compounding over time and creating more barriers with every degree of separation from the genesis of these initial racist structures and the system itself. And in our current era, where the entire country is faced with the coronavirus pandemic as a barrier to learning and where student learning is dependent on access to Wi-Fi and a mobile device, the lack of access to these critical technologies has created yet another barrier for Students of Color and working-class families that is, without a doubt, an extension of the policies and structures created by our racist system.

The solution to this problem was never to have our teachers return to in-person learning prematurely. Due to the easy transmission of COVID-19, it was clear, even to those in favor of returning to school in-person, that convening in large groups would result in the transmission of COVID-19 to teachers and students, resulting in severe illness or even death for some. No, the solution was always—and will always be—to adequately and equitably fund our education system, as well as the systems that support education so that students are no longer subjected to the compounding effects of systemic inequity, and so we can right the wrongs that a white supremacist system has inflicted upon People of Color in our country. If schools and their ancillary systems were funded equitably to support our most vulnerable citizens, we would not be faced with such problems related to childcare, affordable housing, access to food, and access to health care on such a grand scale. Likewise, we would not be faced with a Digital Divide, where Students of Color and working-class students are disproportionately punished simply because they lack access to the internet and mobile devices needed to learn from a distance—resources that can and should be provided by an education system maintained by the wealthiest nation ever to exist in the history of the world.

WEB-BASED LEARNING AS A MEANS OF OPPRESSION

The 2020 California Alliance of Researchers for Equity in Education (CARE-ED) Research Brief also made note of student attitudes toward digital learning, as well as differences in pedagogy, noting that "school districts in high-poverty areas were less likely to offer online instruction to all of their students, and when offered, the instruction was far less likely to be synchronous," suggesting the opposite for affluent areas, that instead, online instruction was more likely to be synchronous. It's no surprise, then, that the same report noted that students from low-income families reported negative attitudes toward learning online and were less likely to engage.

The compounding effects of systemic inequity are evident in our pedagogy, too. While my goal here is not to place blame on teachers for using inequitable practices, it is true that we *all* must look at the role we play in education as oppressors. Because it is impossible to entirely divorce ourselves from the system, and because the system is inextricably connected to the ways in which we think, act, and interact with our students and colleagues, we must critically examine our practice and dismantle any practices that operate in opposition to educational equity.

While I want to challenge every educator to evaluate their pedagogy, I also don't want educators to feel indicted as a result of this self-examination. We are part of a system that institutionalizes children and teachers, one that measures their worth with big data such as norm-referenced standardized assessments, created in response to the demands of a white supremacist society that values quantitative over qualitative metrics. These metrics have had a profound impact on the way we teach; they have incentivized us to take the shortest path possible to most desirable results, which in many schools across the country, translate into higher test scores so our schools look good on paper, increase home values, and perpetuate cycles of privilege, power, and oppression.

Personally, when I reflect on my practice and realize I've been doing something problematic or inequitable, I can't help but feel a deep sense of guilt and shame. I take things very personally, and my discomfort grabs me ruthlessly, sometimes to the point of disengagement. But we must remember that by completely disengaging and no longer reflecting on the inequitable practices we perpetuate in our classrooms, we do further harm. We can, in fact, aim to repair the harm we've caused and restore humanity to our classrooms by reflecting on these problematic practices, using this moment in time as an opportunity for growth and innovation.

As Zaretta Hammond reminds us, any tool or practice that engenders dependence in students is oppressive (2014). In the last chapter, we discussed how many forms of traditional pedagogy mirror the characteristics of white supremacy, and while I could go further in-depth on why didactic curriculum manuals, multiple-choice assessments, and worksheets are examples of oppressive pedagogy, I am choosing to focus on just one form of oppressive digital pedagogy: web-based, adaptive tools marketed for "personalized learning."

"Educational technologies tend to build on the resources of high-performing schools, whereas they tend to distract from the mission and compound the challenges of under-resourced schools," the CARE-ED Research Brief (2020) explains, a phenomenon known as the "Law of Amplification."

It is within the context of personalized learning platforms, guided by digital algorithms instead of sentient educators, that we unearth a second Digital Divide—with some students receiving humanized digital instruction that maximizes synchronous learning blocks, while others receive dehumanizing digital instruction, often asynchronous, that emphasizes work completion and minutes spent on web-based, adaptive programs. These digital programs, as we discussed in the Chapter 8, that adapt to a child's "level," provide educators and administrators alike with the very thing that free-market capitalism has taught them to desire—the shortest path possible to the most desirable results, which in this case, hopefully translates into high test scores. It's comes as no surprise when web-based, adaptive personalized learning programs translate into higher test scores. Students are likely to perform better on multiple-choice standardized assessments when they spend a disproportionate amount of their learning time on adaptive programs that directly mirror those standardized assessments.

However, many schools fail to consider the long-term effects of these sorts of programs. They don't teach for independence, free thought, or student liberation. These programs, instead, teach to institutionalize; they teach in the interest of efficient content consumption, engendering mindlessness and dependence in our students. They teach in a way that resembles a business, minimizing costs and maximizing profits in the form of test scores. As a result, students quickly learn that they are not subjects of an educational narrative that will allow them to liberate themselves; they learn they are the objects of an education system looking to further use them as tools of free-market capitalism later in life. It's no wonder students have negative attitudes about online learning when they're forced to learn in a manner that robs them of their humanity.

At first glance, these programs seem like an excellent choice for distance learning—and it's because many of us are conditioned to believe that this is what learning should be, a tool for getting a job or getting ahead. When teaching from a distance, these tools may, in fact, seem like they can solve our problems for differentiation by minimizing the complexity of individualizing instruction. But the reality is that they create more problems than they solve. While they may minimize the complexity of individualizing content consumption, they make teachers' jobs more complex, causing them to sift through meaningless quantitative data, all the while dehumanizing our students in the process. This is why we must take a minimalist—and humanist—approach to integrating technology into our classrooms. This breed of education technology, while marketed as a panacea for educational equity, is only exacerbating systemic inequity; it's only dehumanizing our students, when our approach to teaching and learning, no matter where we are, should be allowing our students to become all the more human through the process of learning.

TIPS FOR TEACHING FROM A DISTANCE, CHAPTER 9

- Consider the fact that all of your students may not have equal access to internet or devices.

- Stay politically involved and vote for policies that support systemic change in education and the systems that support education, including changing the way our schools are funded.

- Teach in a manner that makes your students conscious of the system they're living in. When students are conscious of the systems they live in, they are more conscious of oppression and how to dismantle it.

- Use digital pedagogy responsibly. Do not put students on web-based, adaptive programs. Maximize synchronous learning and social connectedness.

CHAPTER TEN

CENTERING HUMANITY

I'll ask one more time: Shouldn't we always, in some ways, be teaching from a distance? Shouldn't we always be teaching with liberation in mind, and in a manner that allows our students to stand on their own?

No, this is not an endorsement of asynchronous learning where we leave students to fend for themselves in an era of distance learning, and likewise, this isn't my recommendation for a radical model of individualism where students learn what, how, and when they want. Instead, it's an impetus to reposition ourselves in the classroom—a reminder that we do our best teaching when we guide our students from the side; when we sit by, observe them, and humanize our assessment practices; when we take steps to actively remove the barriers that systemic inequities create for our students. It's a call to action—and a gentle nudge—to reflect mindfully on your practice and use this moment in time to innovate, cast aside archaic practices, and center your students' humanity like never before. Because if we're especially honest with ourselves, far too many pedagogies that numerous teachers were employing prior to the start pandemic—practices that center industrialized curricula like worksheets and web-based adaptive programs or the high-stakes standardized assessments that were imposed on us—were dehumanizing and operating in opposition to student liberation.

Oddly enough, it wasn't even quality pedagogy that offered the most compelling argument for returning to school in person. It was, instead, an argument for socialization and in-person social connection. To many, it seemed impossible to socialize over our computers; it seemed impossible to form connections and build community while learning through screens. Alas, we have ample evidence to suggest otherwise. Powerful technologies like video conferencing and social media have made the world a smaller place, allowing us to, in fact, form connections with those near and far from us, separated by multiple time zones and worlds of cultural difference. Given the realities and powers of digital technology, distance learning can absolutely be a viable alternative for socialization and centering humanity in times of crisis—especially if it means saving human lives.

I was reminded of this on the final day of my tenth year of teaching. As I've mentioned, the transition to distance learning wasn't easy, and as a result, part of me was ready to breathe a sigh of relief once I signed off for the last time. In other ways, I had grown accustomed to teaching from home. It was nice to wake up a bit later over the past few months; in some ways, it was rejuvenating to be able to teach from home, to pee when I wanted to, and to be relieved of the mundane and undesirable responsibilities of teaching. Gone, it seemed, were the days of quieting my students down in the hall-ways, of dealing with the lunchroom drama and the exasperated sighs I'd release after having to try and retry our transition from our tables to the door.

But part of me also felt a deep sense of sadness to be ending the year this way. Gone, too, were the joyful explosions of voices during writing workshop, the eruption of laughter when we just couldn't keep our giggles inside, and the incalculable, indescribable, but also unforgettable feeling of simply being *together*, bonded through the mere proximity of sharing the same physical space for the better part of a year and the majority of our waking hours. It's humbling to realize just how much being *in person* matters when teaching. So much of what we do hinges upon our ability to look into each other's eyes, to read the room and one another's body language.

But sacrificing in-person learning was all with good reason. We made these sacrifices because we had to—and we should continue to do so in times when it's necessary. COVID-19 took us all by surprise, and I would happily do an entire additional year of distance learning in order to prevent more Americans from becoming critically ill and losing their lives.

Perhaps there will always be a silver lining to this era of teaching and learning. For me, it renewed my appreciation for the humanity of teaching; it reminded me to bring my students' and my own humanity to the center of teaching and learning quite possibly more than I ever had. It reminded me that, even in the darkest of days when the mind-numbing reality of staring at a screen all day set in yet again, that being flexible with my schedule and finding ways to connect with my students gave me the energy I needed to get through the day.

FLEXIBLE SCHEDULING

In the first weeks of distance learning, I inevitably noticed that I was losing a couple of my students. As I mentioned in Chapter 3, I tried to operate from a place of trust with my students. When they didn't want to have their cameras on, I honored that. I understood how intimidating it was to be on display for an entire group of people, and I also knew that some of my students felt as though their privacy was being invaded by having a camera look directly into their homes. But there was one student, among many, who I knew struggled with executive functioning, who often presented as distractible, and who otherwise had trouble regulating his body and his mind to attend to academic tasks and learn with independence—even when we were learning in person. The work Kayden turned in on Seesaw demonstrated this, too. It looked as though he completed it as quickly as possible, despite the fact that I required students to stay in our synchronous learning sessions for the entire scheduled duration.

Naturally, I set up a call with his parents, not as a means for punishment or shaming, but instead to inquire about their experience with distance learning thus far and how they felt Kayden was handling this significant change. I soon learned that distance learning had been especially challenging for him and his family. Both parents had jobs that were in especially high demand beginning in March.

"He's really struggling," they told me. "He's craving structure and connection."

My heart broke talking to the family. It was clear that Kayden needed some extra support, not necessarily with academic skills or mastering academic content. He just needed some time to connect.

Fortunately, I had built a flexible hour into my schedule each day, a time which I called "office hours," allowing me to work with students one-on-one for various academic interventions. In Kayden's case, however, this would not be an academic intervention; it would be an intervention to provide him the connection and structure he was craving. I posed an idea to his parents: What if I set Kayden up with a passion project? Could an appropriately structured independent project provide a little extra structure for Kayden along with an additional opportunity to connect with me? Kayden's parents expressed excitement at the idea, and luckily, so did Kayden.

Every day thereafter, for the remainder of the school year, Kayden showed up right on time, promptly at 8:00 a.m., to check in with me, talk for a few minutes, and then begin work on his passion project. In the classroom, he always had been industrious and passionate about learning. He loved to explore words, and it was a common occurrence for him to run up to me asking lots of questions about the topics we were studying in class. His passion for learning was inextinguishable, and it became clear quite quickly that he wasn't going to let a global pandemic get in the way of that.

We used a kanban board, a tool I began using in San Francisco when I used to build passion projects with my students as a part of my plan for personalizing learning. The kanban board was originally developed by Toyota as a manufacturing process, helping break down complex projects into steps (Gross & McInnis, 2003). I hadn't had an opportunity to try passion projects after my move back to Chicago, but I couldn't have thought of a better opportunity to give them a whirl once again.

As we've discussed at length in this book, our goal for students should always be independence, and this is one of the reasons I use the kanban board tool (see Figure 10.1). It not only builds executive functioning skills which are critical to independence, it creates a structure in which students can execute the many steps of a project on their own, leaning on the adult in the room for assistance when necessary, as opposed to overrelying on them to keep the project going.

Kayden was very amenable to the idea of the kanban board, as I was very explicit about why we were using it.

"You know me by now," I said to him. "Why do I want you to be independent?"

"Because you want me to be able to learn on my own!"

"Exactly," I replied. I would always tell them during the school year that I wasn't doing my job correctly if I was doing everything for them. The easier thing for me to do, I would say, would be to simply tell them the answers and give them the quickest strategy for solving problems. I choose the harder approach—helping them figure it out for themselves—because I care about them. I was glad the message had stuck. It was clear Kayden was ready for a new tool that would aid his independence.

Figure 10.1: Kayden's Kanban Board

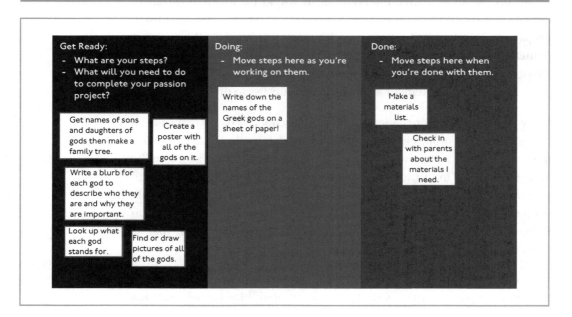

You'll notice that kanban board shown in Figure 10.1 is structured using the Get Ready, Do, Done structure, created by speech and language pathologists Kristen Jacobsen and Sarah Ward (2016). Get Ready, Do, Done builds executive functioning skills by training students to break down a task or process into steps. I used a simple Google Slides file to create the different sections of the board. The movable cards were white rectangles. By double-clicking on them, Kayden was able to insert text in them and duplicate them to make more. Not only was this tool easy to make, it was easy for Kayden to manipulate and share his progress with me since I constantly had access to the document. It was also easy to copy, in the event that I wanted to use it with other students.

It wasn't long before Kayden was up and running, excited to do research on Greek gods, a topic he had picked after being captivated by the *Percy Jackson* series. He decided he wanted to use Book Creator to make a book about the family of Greek gods he was researching.

A few weeks later, when he shared his newly created book with my co-teacher and me, pride poured out of him. He was thrilled to share his final work product with us, not only because it was about a topic he loved—but also because he'd done it on his own. Selfishly, I like to think that part of his joy had to do with the extra time he had to connect with his teachers, early in the mornings when none of his peers seemed to want to be online.

This example of Kayden and his kanban board speaks to the importance of building in unstructured times when engaging in distance learning. Engaging with our humanity and giving it space to breathe is messy and unpredictable. Student agency is, too. Without these flexible times where I came to our virtual classroom with no agenda other than wanting to connect with students, meet them where they were, and otherwise provide assistance where they needed it, I would not have been able to add this personal touch to distance learning.

FINDING WAYS TO CONNECT

"So what do you all want to do with our last week of school?" I asked the grid of faces before me.

Students started writing ideas in the chat. They wanted to read stories, share their writing, and otherwise do the typical things that we might do in the last week of school.

"How about a talent show?" one student suggested.

At first, I'll admit, I was a little skeptical.

"Tell me a little bit more," I asked.

So many of the students in my class loved music, and in a week or so, I would learn just how talented they all were. A handful of them mentioned they historically participated in a talent show in music class, but due to the pandemic, they were unable to this year. It was one of their last wishes for the school year to share one last piece of themselves.

I consented to this unconventional, yet exciting idea, and before I knew it, it was the morning of my first-ever student-led talent show, conducted entirely virtually. Students recorded themselves playing their musical instruments while some played live; others had made funny movie trailers on iMovie while some showed videos of them doing a gymnastics routine or playing a sport they loved. My co-teacher shared some of her art she'd been working on at home, and even I was able to play one of my favorite songs and sing along.

Tears stung behind my eyes as I sang the lyrics of "Leader of the Band," an old folk song by Dan Fogelberg (1981), an ode and goodbye to a metaphorical father figure:

> I thank you for the music, and your stories of the road.
>
> I thank you for my freedom when it came my time to go.
>
> I thank you for the kindness, and the times when you talked tough.
>
> But Papa, I don't think I said, I loved you near enough.

Perhaps on a subconscious level I knew that this would be my last time being a teacher in a real, live classroom for a while—for just a few months later, I would resign from my teaching position, refusing to subject myself to the dangers of in-person learning in the midst of a global pandemic. Perhaps it was just the ache of disconnection I was feeling, not having been able to set foot in a classroom and feel the energy of twenty-one students needing me. Regardless, this moment in time, conjured up entirely by my wonderful students, made it possible for me to continue to connect and bond with them, up until the very last note. The piano echoed in the tiny office from which I'd taught for the preceding two months, and my students erupted in applause at my amateur musicality. At the end of the day, it didn't matter how talented any of us actually were. What mattered most was that we found a way to make the best of a bad situation. We found a way to connect when the rest of the world was telling us that human connection and socialization weren't possible through distance learning.

I can't help but think that this sort of defeatist thinking about the limited possibilities of distance learning comes from the narrow way that we define learning within the limits of a white supremacist, patriarchal culture. There are, in fact, so many ways to learn from a distance, but we've conditioned ourselves to believe that we need to have a teacher right next to us in order for learning to occur, controlling our every move and dictating our every thought. But there are innumerable examples from both the present and past that disprove this and beckon us to redefine what learning is in the COVID era and beyond. We read books written by authors long gone and far away—and we manage to feel connected to them through the timeless lessons they teach us through their writing. Videos go viral on social media, uniting strangers through collective outrage, joy, and laughter. Thanks to the miracle of the internet, we've managed to stay connected to our families, friends, and colleagues through the apparition of our bodies into each other's homes, albeit in digital format. There is, in fact, a great deal of possibility in the potential of distance learning to serve a distinct purpose. In times of crisis where the risks of learning together in person vastly outweigh the benefits, we can use distance learning to preserve the sense of humanity that a global pandemic has so ruthlessly taken from us—and perhaps even create new possibilities, codifying a new vision for what learning looks like when humanity is put front and center.

A NEW VISION FOR TEACHING AND LEARNING

That day of the talent show, unknowingly my last day of traditional school for what would be the foreseeable future, I read my favorite book, *The Three Questions* (2002) by Jon J. Muth. I told myself I'd keep my emotions in control; I told myself I wouldn't cry. But as I approached the final pages of the story and conveyed to my students the importance of doing right by the ones who stand beside us and that the most important time will always be the present, I realized I couldn't keep it in anymore. The sides of my mouth curled up and my voice began to shake. It became clear to me in that moment that I was just as connected to my students in this virtual classroom as I had been in person. The feeling of connectedness and our sense of community was too strong to be challenged by the obstacles of distance learning.

I came to the end of the story, said one final goodbye, and watched each of their little rectangles disappear from the grid. I felt a familiar feeling—that feeling of loneliness I always feel on the last day of school, brought about by the deafening silence of a classroom without any children in it. It turns out it wasn't that much different—even if we were saying goodbye from a distance.

I hope you see the stories I've shared within this book as a provocation—a provocation for a new way of teaching and learning that can be actualized from a distance, but that could also be realized when it is safe enough for all of us to be back in person, learning from the boundless energy that a lively classroom of students brings us.

We teach—and we learn—not for the sake of growing the American economy or to maintain a perceived sense of American exceptionalism: we teach and we learn because it is part of the human condition, ingrained in our DNA through generations of human beings who pursued something greater than themselves, something that transcended space, time, and perhaps even their own existence.

The sad reality is that we've lost sight of the true purpose of education, and it is our collective reckoning as a result of distance learning that has made this especially clear. We stand on the precipice of great change in our country and in our world. We see the immediate effects of climate change bearing down on us; we see the damage and heartache that our complicity in systemic racism has caused all of us, but primarily People of Color in the United States; we better understand the fragility of our democracy and the terror that authoritarian politics strikes within us; and we now can see even more acutely how dehumanizing our education system has become, partially due to systemic inequities but also through the archaic practices, reminiscent of white supremacist and patriarchal thinking, that limit our students' liberation.

I want to emphasize one last time that this book is not meant to be an indictment of teachers and teaching. I recognize that teachers work within systems and that those systems have constraints. But the problems that distance learning has brought about are not due to distance learning itself; they're due to the fact that the systemic and pedagogical problems we see now were more easily shielded or ignored while teachers and students were behind brick walls and closed doors. Now that they're on display for everyone to see, it's exceedingly clear that we have to reimagine pedagogy—and the education system at-large. I have hope that we will do so.

Privatization advocates are hopeful that the COVID era will create more opportunities for "school choice," as evidenced by Betsy DeVos's desire to funnel money into private and parochial schools shortly after the pandemic hit, but I want to make it clear that when I say reimagine the education system, I mean equitably fund *public* education and invest in the teachers, staff, and students who breathe life into our public school system.

The push for school choice is yet another manifestation of free-market capitalism funneling wealth and privilege to those with the most access and power.

That said, I am optimistic that teachers around the country are seeing this moment as a call to action. But I also know that should we remain constantly vigilant and relentlessly mindful, consciously dismantling practices and structures that reinforce white supremacy or free-market capitalism in our schools. Should we refrain from dismantling these structures, business will continue on as usual, and we'll revert back to the same education system that wasn't working prior to COVID-19. If we allow privatization advocates to have their way, it could get even worse.

To learn is to be human; to learn is to humanize others and ourselves, and I believe that if we center humanity and equity in every decision we make, we can reimagine our schools and our school systems in the image of all those who enter it. If and when we center humanity and equity, we can remind ourselves that all human beings have value, and that it is our collective responsibility to care for one another, to share power through partnership, and perhaps even give up some of the power that our privilege brings us, in whatever way it manifests.

In sum, teaching from a distance—and teaching for student liberation—ultimately entails sharing our power as educators. In the context of a white supremacist, patriarchal system, hoarding power inevitably results in the dehumanization of others, and so in order to center humanity in our classrooms, we must share our power with our students. We must build strong classroom communities that allow students to show up in their full humanity; we must teach them how to learn, centering socioemotional literacy, executive functioning skills, and identity; we must teach in a way that allows them to openly engage in dialogue with their peers, and we must help them reflect productively on their learning with qualitative assessment; and finally, we must find ways to dismantle policies, structures, and practices that limit our students' independence.

The COVID crisis is neither the first nor the last time that humanity will be in a time of crisis. It's happened before, and it will inevitably happen again. Our humanity will *always* be at stake, and as a result, we must remember that our collective purpose for teaching must always be to humanize—to teach and learn in the pursuit of a deeper sense of collective humanity—and to do so not for economic means, but for the inclusion and empowerment of all students.

TIPS FOR TEACHING FROM A DISTANCE, CHAPTER 10

- Ask your students for input on community-building activities that make them feel more connected to one another.

- Use structures like the kanban board to create individualized passion projects.

- Build flexible times into your schedules, like office hours, where kids can come to check in, get extra help, or connect.

- Center humanity in your decision making, in order continue humanizing learning.

REFERENCES

INTRODUCTION

Abolitionist teaching and the future of our schools [Video file]. (2020, June 23). https://www.youtube.com/watch?v=uJZ3RPJ2rNc

Coates, T. (2014, June). *The case for reparations.* https://www.theatlantic.com/magazine/archive/2014/06/the-case-for-reparations/361631/

Freire, P., & Ramos, M. B. (1970). *Pedagogy of the oppressed.* Seabury Press.

Gladwell, M. (Host). (2017, June 28). *Miss Buchanan's period of adjustment* [Audio Podcast]. Retrieved from http://revisionisthistory.com/episodes/13-miss-buchanans-period-of-adjustment

Kendi, I. X. (2019). *How to be an anti-racist.* Penguin.

Saad, L. (2020). *Me and white supremacy: Combat racism, change the world, and become a good ancestor.* Sourcebooks.

CHAPTER 1

Hammond, Z. (2014). *Culturally responsive teaching and the brain.* Corwin.

Hattie, J. (2017). *Visible Learning Plus: 250 influences on student achievement.* https://visible-learning.org/wp-content/uploads/2018/03/VLPLUS-252-Influences-Hattie-ranking-DEC-2017.pdf

Jones, K., & Okun, T. (2001). *Dismantling racism: A workbook for social change groups.* ChangeWork.

National Equity Project. (2020). *Social emotional learning and equity.* https://www.nationalequityproject.org/frameworks/social-emotional-learning-and-equity

Okun, T., & Jones, K. (2001). *Dismantling racism: A workbook for social change groups.* ChangeWork.

Saad, L. (2020). *Me and white supremacy: Combat racism, change the world, and become a good ancestor.* Sourcebooks.

CHAPTER 2

Calkins, L., & Tolan, K. (2015). *Research clubs: Elephants, penguins, and frogs, oh my! Units of study for teaching reading: A workshop curriculum*, Grades K–5. Heinemann Press.

DeGruy, J. (2005). *Post-traumatic slave syndrome.* Uptone Press.

Kuypers, L. (2011). *Zones of Regulation.* Think Social.

Madda, M. (2019). *Dena Simmons: Without context, social-emotional learning can backfire.* https://www.edsurge.com/news/2019-05-15-dena-simmons-without-context-social-emotional-learning-can-backfire

Oluo, I. (2019). *So you want to talk about race?* Seal Press.

Teaching Tolerance Staff. (2020). *A trauma-informed approach to teaching through coronavirus.* https://www.tolerance.org/magazine/a-trauma-informed-approach-to-teaching-through-coronavirus

CHAPTER 3

France, P. (2019). *Reclaiming personalized learning: A pedagogy for restoring equity and humanity in our classrooms.* Corwin.

Ladson-Billings, G. (1994). *The dreamkeepers: Successful teachers of African-American children.* Jossey-Bass.

Milner, H. R., Cunningham, H. B., Delale-O'Connor, L., & Kestenberg, E. G. (2019). *"These kids are out of control": Why we must reimagine "classroom management" for equity.* Corwin.

Responsive Classroom. (2015). *The first six weeks of school.* Center for Responsive Schools.

CHAPTER 4

Buckner, A. (2005). *Notebook know-how: Strategies for the writer's notebook.* Stenhouse.

Calkins, L., Frazin, S., & Roberts, M. B. (2013). *Once upon a time, units of study for teaching reading: A workshop curriculum, grades K–5.* Heinemann Press.

Cole, B. (1987). *Prince Cinders.* Puffin Books.

Common Core State Standards Initiative. (2020). http://www.corestandards.org/

Dietz, M. (2000). *Single-point rubric idea.* Presented at INTASC Academy, July 12–21, Alverno College, Milwaukee, Wisconsin.

Fluckiger, J. (2010). Single point rubric: A tool for responsible student self-assessment. Teacher Education Faculty Publications. 5. https://digitalcommons.unomaha.edu/tedfacpub/5

Garcia Winner, M. (2008). *Think social! A social-thinking curriculum for school age students.* Think Social.

Gonzalez, J. (2015, February 15). *Meet the single point rubric.* https://www.cultofpedagogy.com/single-point-rubric/

Gottlieb, M. (2016). *Assessing English language learners: Bridges to educational equity: Connecting academic language proficiency to student achievement.* Corwin.

Hyerle, D. (1995). *Thinking maps: Tools for learning.* Innovative Learning Group.

Muhammad, G. (2020). *Cultivating genius: An equity framework for culturally and historically responsive literacy.* Scholastic.

Teaching Tolerance. (2019). Social Justice Standards. https://www.tolerance.org/frameworks/social-justice-standards

Wiggins, G., & McTighe, J. (2005). *Understanding by design.* ASCD.

CHAPTER 5

Adichie, C. N. (2009). *The danger of a single story* [Video file]. https://www.ted.com/talks/chimamanda_ngozi_adichie_the_danger_of_a_single_story?language=en

Ahmed, S. (2018). *Being the change: Lessons and strategies to teach social comprehension.* Pearson Education.

Common Core State Standards Initiative. (2020). http://www.corestandards.org/

Hyerle, D. (1995). *Thinking maps: Tools for learning.* Innovative Learning Group.

Ladson-Billings, G. (1994). *The dreamkeepers: Successful teachers of African-American children.* Jossey-Bass.

Penfold, A., & Kaufman, S. (2018). *All are welcome.* Bloomsbury.

Ritchhart, R., Church, M., & Morrison, K. (2011). *Making thinking visible: How to promote engagement, understanding, and independence for all learners*. Jossey-Bass.

Teaching Tolerance. (2019). *Social Justice Standards*. https://www.tolerance.org/frameworks/social-justice-standards

Wiggins, G., & McTighe, J. (2005). *Understanding by design*. ASCD.

CHAPTER 6

Calkins, L., Frazin, S., & Roberts, M. B. (2013). *Once upon a time, units of study for teaching reading: A workshop curriculum, grades K–5*. Heinemann Press.

Calkins, L., & Tolan, K. (2015). *Research clubs: Elephants, penguins, and frogs, oh my! Units of study for teaching reading: A workshop curriculum, grades K–5*. Heinemann Press.

Campbell, D. T. (1979). Assessing the impact of planned social change. *Evaluation and Program Planning, 2*(1), 67–90.

CASEL. (2020). https://casel.org/

Common Core State Standards Initiative. (2020). http://www.corestandards.org/

Dietz, M. (2000). *Single-point rubric idea*. Presented at INTASC Academy, July 12–21, Alverno College, Milwaukee, Wisconsin.

Fluckiger, J. *Single point rubric: A tool for responsible student self-assessment*. (2010). Teacher Education Faculty Publications. 5. https://digitalcommons.unomaha.edu/tedfacpub/5

Gonzalez, J. (2015, February 15). *Meet the single point rubric*. https://www.cultofpedagogy.com/single-point-rubric/

Gottlieb, M. (2016). *Assessing English language learners: Bridges to educational equity: Connecting academic language proficiency to student achievement*. Corwin.

Muhammad, G. (2020). *Cultivating genius: An equity framework for culturally and historically responsive literacy*. Scholastic.

National Council for the Social Studies. (2017, June). *The College, Career, and Civic Life (C3) Framework for Social Studies State Standards: Guidance for enhancing the rigor of K–12 civics, economics, geography, and history*. https://www.socialstudies.org/sites/default/files/c3/c3-framework-for-social-studies-rev0617.pdf

Next Generation Science Standards. (2020). https://www.nextgenscience.org/

Okun, T., & Jones, K. (2001). *Dismantling racism: A workbook for social change groups*. Changework.

Pett, M., & Rubenstein, G. (2011). *The girl who never made mistakes*. Sourcebooks.

Pink, D. (2011). *Drive: The surprising truth about what motivates us*. Riverhead Books.

Teaching Tolerance. (2019). *Social Justice Standards*. https://www.tolerance.org/frameworks/social-justice-standards

Wood, C. (2007). *Yardsticks: Children in the classroom ages 4–14*. Northeast Foundation for Children.

CHAPTER 7

Buckner, A. (2005). *Notebook know-how: Strategies for the writer's notebook*. Stenhouse.

Cohen E., & Lotan, R. (1997). *Working for equity in heterogeneous classrooms: Sociological theory in practice*. Teachers College Press.

Hyerle, D. (1995). *Thinking maps: Tools for learning*. Innovative Learning Group.

Okun, T., & Jones, K. (2001). *Dismantling racism: A workbook for social change groups.* Changework.

Pearson, P. D., & Gallagher, M. (1983, October). The instruction of reading comprehension. *Contemporary Educational Psychology, 8*(3), 317–344.

Ritchhart, R., Church, M., & Morrison, K. (2011). Making thinking visible: How to promote engagement, understanding, and independence for all learners. Jossey-Bass.

Routman, R. (2004). *Writing essentials: Raising expectations and results while simplifying teaching.* Heinemann Press.

CHAPTER 8

American Academy of Pediatrics. (2016). Media use in school-aged children and adolescents. *Pediatrics, 128*(5), 1040th ser. https://pediatrics.aappublications.org/content/138/5/e20162592

France, P. (2019). *Reclaiming personalized learning: A pedagogy for restoring equity and humanity in our classrooms.* Corwin.

Gottlieb, M. (2016). *Assessing English language learners: Bridges to educational equity: Connecting academic language proficiency to student achievement.* Corwin.

Jones, K., & Okun, T. (2001). *Dismantling racism: A workbook for social change groups.* ChangeWork.

Pearson, P. D., & Gallagher, M. (1983, October). The instruction of reading comprehension. *Contemporary Educational Psychology, 8(3),* 317–344.

Rifkin, J. (2010). *The empathic civilization.* Penguin Books.

Sweetser, P., Johnson, D., Ozdowska, A., & Wyeth, P. (2012). Active versus passive screen time for young children. *Australasian Journal of Early Childhood, 37*(4). https://journals.sagepub.com/doi/abs/10.1177/183693911203700413

CHAPTER 9

Baldwin, J. (1963, December 21). A Talk to Teachers. *The Saturday Review.*

California Alliance of Researchers for Equity in Education. (2020). *The shift to online education during and beyond the COVID-19 pandemic: Concerns and recommendations for California.* http://www.care-ed.org

Centers for Disease Control and Prevention. (2020, September). *Health disparities: Race and Hispanic origin.* https://www.cdc.gov/nchs/nvss/vsrr/covid19/health_disparities.htm

Chandra, S., Chang, A., Day, L., Fazlullah, A., Liu, J., McBride, L., Mudalige, T., & Weiss, D. (2020). *Closing the K–12 digital divide in the age of distance learning.* Common Sense Media.

Coates, T. (2014, June). *The case for reparations.* https://www.theatlantic.com/magazine/archive/2014/06/the-case-for-reparations/361631/

Gladwell, M. (Host). (2017, June 28). *Miss Buchanan's period of adjustment* [Audio Podcast]. Retrieved from http://revisionisthistory.com/episodes/13-miss-buchanans-period-of-adjustment

Hammond, Z. (2014). *Culturally responsive teaching and the brain.* Corwin.

Home Owners' Loan Corporation. (1939). *Residential security map.* https://www.theatlantic.com/magazine/archive/2014/06/the-case-for-reparations/361631/

Illinois State Report Card. (2019a). *CITY OF CHICAGO SD 299 | Per student spending*. https://www.illinoisreportcard.com/district.aspx?source=environment&source2=perstudentspending&Districtid=15016299025

Illinois State Report Card. (2019b). *CITY OF CHICAGO SD 299 | Racial/ethnic diversity*. https://www.illinoisreportcard.com/district.aspx?source=studentcharacteristics&source2=studentdemographics&Districtid=15016299025

Illinois State Report Card. (2019c). *OAK PARK & RIVER FOREST HIGH SC | Per student spending*. https://www.illinoisreportcard.com/school.aspx?source=environment&source2=perstudentspending&Schoolid=060162000130001

Illinois State Report Card. (2019d). *OAK PARK & RIVER FOREST HIGH SC | Racial/ethnic diversity*. https://www.illinoisreportcard.com/school.aspx?source=studentcharacteristics&source2=studentdemographics&Schoolid=060162000130001

Johnson, S. (2018, September 26). *Story of Oak Park fending off 'white flight' is told in frank detail at new village history museum*. https://www.chicagotribune.com/entertainment/museums/ct-ent-oak-park-history-museum-0927-story.html

Kendi, I. X. (2019). *How to be an anti-racist*. Penguin.

Kumashiro, K. (2012). *Bad teacher! How blaming teachers distorts the bigger picture*. Teachers College Press.

National Center for Education Statistics. (2020, May). *Racial/ethnic enrollment in public schools*. https://nces.ed.gov/programs/coe/indicator_cge.asp

Reschovsky, A. (2017). *The future of U.S. public school revenue from the property tax*. Re https://www.lincolninst.edu/sites/default/files/pubfiles/future-us-public-school-revenue-policy-brief_0.pdf

U.S. Census Bureau. (2019, July). *Quick facts: United States*. https://www.census.gov/quickfacts/fact/table/US/PST045219

WATCH: Michelle Obama's full speech at the Democratic National Convention | 2020 DNC Night 1 [Video file]. (2020, August 17). https://www.youtube.com/watch?v=uKy3iiWjhVI

Woods, H. (2020, August 3). *How billionaires got $637 billion richer during the coronavirus pandemic*. https://www.businessinsider.com/billionaires-net-worth-increases-coronavirus-pandemic-2020-7

CHAPTER 10

Gross, J. M., & McInnis, K. R. (2003). *Kanban made simple—Demystifying and applying Toyota's legendary manufacturing process*. Amacom.

Fogelberg, D. (1981). "The Leader of the Band." *The Innocent Age*. Full Moon/Epic.

Muth, J. J. (2002). *The three questions*. Scholastic Press.

Ward, S., & Jacobsen, K. (2016). *Strategies for improving executive function skills to plan, organize, and problem solve for school success*. http://www.glenbardgps.org/wp-content/uploads/2016/06/sarah-ward-executive-function-lecture-handout-December-6-2016-Glenbard-IL.pdf

INDEX

Figures are indicated by f following the page number.

A SAGE Publishing Company

Helping educators make the greatest impact

CORWIN HAS ONE MISSION: to enhance education through intentional professional learning.

We build long-term relationships with our authors, educators, clients, and associations who partner with us to develop and continuously improve the best evidence-based practices that establish and support lifelong learning.

Solutions YOU WANT | Experts YOU TRUST | Results YOU NEED

EVENTS

>>> INSTITUTES

Corwin Institutes provide large regional events where educators collaborate with peers and learn from industry experts. Prepare to be recharged and motivated!

corwin.com/institutes

ON-SITE PD

>>> ON-SITE PROFESSIONAL LEARNING

Corwin on-site PD is delivered through high-energy keynotes, practical workshops, and custom coaching services designed to support knowledge development and implementation.

corwin.com/pd

>>> PROFESSIONAL DEVELOPMENT RESOURCE CENTER

The PD Resource Center provides school and district PD facilitators with the tools and resources needed to deliver effective PD.

corwin.com/pdrc

ONLINE

>>> ADVANCE

Designed for K–12 teachers, Advance offers a range of online learning options that can qualify for graduate-level credit and apply toward license renewal.

corwin.com/advance

Contact a PD Advisor at (800) 831-6640 or visit www.corwin.com for more information